ungrafted

SOUTHERN MESSENGER POETS

Dave Smith, Series Editor

ungrafted

New and Selected Poems

Claudia Emerson

LOUISIANA STATE UNIVERSITY PRESS
BATON ROUGE

Published with the assistance of the Sea Cliff Fund

Published by Louisiana State University Press
lsupress.org

Manufactured in the United States of America
First printing

DESIGNER: Barbara Neely Bourgoyne
TYPEFACE: Whitman
PRINTER AND BINDER: Sheridan Books, Inc.

Jacket/cover illustration: Adobe Stock/javier_garcia.

Of the previously uncollected poems, "Single Shot," "Face Blindness," "The Bookmobile Lady," and "Eschatologies" first appeared in *Blackbird*. "Red Sam in the Days That Follow," "Lucynell in Heaven," and "Joy in the Loft" first appeared in *Shenandoah*. "Ungrafted: Jefferson's Vines" first appeared in *Monticello in Mind: Fifty Contemporary Poems on Jefferson*, ed. Lisa Russ Spaar (University of Virginia Press, 2016).

LIBRARY OF CONGRESS CATALOGING-IN-PUBLICATION DATA
Names: Emerson, Claudia, 1957–2014, author.
Title: Ungrafted : new and selected poems / Claudia Emerson.
Other titles: Ungrafted (Compilation)
Description: Baton Rouge : Louisiana State University Press, [2025] | Series: Southern messenger poets
Identifiers: LCCN 2024033206 (print) | LCCN 2024033207 (ebook) | ISBN 978-0-8071-8279-6 (paperback) | ISBN 978-0-8071-8358-8 (cloth) | ISBN 978-0-8071-8357-1 (pdf) | ISBN 978-0-8071-8356-4 (epub)
Subjects: LCGFT: Poetry.
Classification: LCC PS3551.N4155 U54 2025 (print) | LCC PS3551.N4155 (ebook) | DDC 811/.54—dc23/eng/20240930
LC record available at https://lccn.loc.gov/2024033206
LC ebook record available at https://lccn.loc.gov/2024033207

contents

UNGRAFTED: NEW POEMS

3 Cistern
4 Single Shot
5 Woman Humming
7 Low Sunday
8 Face Blindness
10 Red Sam in the Days That Follow
11 Early Elegy: Thyroid
12 Planer
14 Pitty Sing in Arms
15 Lucynell in Heaven
16 Bus in the Quarry
18 Temporary Madness
19 Joy in the Loft
20 Learning to Dive
22 Jaguar
23 Bachelor-Brother
24 Here nor There: Participant Observations
26 Degrees of Rape
28 The Bookmobile Lady
29 Confession
30 Crawl Space
32 L'Inconnue de la Seine
33 A Mother's Day Poem for Mary, Mother of George
34 Eschatologies

36 A Pastoral
38 Ungrafted: Jefferson's Vines

CLAUDE BEFORE TIME AND SPACE (2018)

41 Swimming Alone
45 The Wheel
47 Pre-Algebra, 1970
50 A Life Beyond
52 On Leaving the Body to Science
55 Midwife
58 Rabbit
60 Rabies
61 Drybridge
63 Before Space

THE OPPOSITE HOUSE (2015)

67 House Sparrows
68 Clearcut
69 Scarecrow at the Forks of Buffalo
70 Charting the Particulars
71 Third
72 Entrance
74 Cursive
75 Smallpox
76 Lock
78 The Opposite House
81 Rural Letter Carrier
83 Common House Sparrows at JFK's International Terminal
84 Virginia Christian
88 The Ocularist

IMPOSSIBLE BOTTLE (2015)

95 MRI
98 Well
99 *Chain Chain Chain*
101 Weather
103 Ornithography: Preparing the Study Skin
105 Blood-Groove
107 Infusion Suite
119 Mortuary Make-Up Artist
120 A Thought
122 Cyst
123 Fast
125 Impossible Bottle
127 The Scar

SECURE THE SHADOW (2012)

131 It
134 Animal Funerals, 1964
136 First Death
138 Zenith
140 Old Elementary
141 Calf Killings
142 Documentary
149 The Present Tense
150 Cause
151 Jubilation
153 For Once
154 Lifeguard
155 Flocking Theory

FIGURE STUDIES (2008)

159 The Mannequin above *Main Street Motors*
160 Latin Teacher
162 Warmbloods
163 Living Nativity
164 Organist
165 Upper Arcade
166 Orchid Anatomy
167 Synchronized Swimming
168 History Lesson
169 *Esto Absoluta*
170 Funny Valentine
171 Old Proof
172 Piano Fire
174 Elevator Operator, Danville, Virginia, 1964
175 Finger of Mercury
177 Photographer
178 At the Route One Flea Market
179 The Medical Venus

LATE WIFE (2005)

183 Natural History Exhibits
185 Photograph: Farm Auction
186 Rent
188 Waxwing
189 Eight Ball
190 Pitching Horseshoes
191 Possessions
192 The Spanish Lover
193 The Change

194 Second Bearing, 1919
196 The Audubon Collection
198 The Practice Cage
200 Atlas
202 Artifact
203 Pond Turtle
204 The Cough
205 Driving Glove
206 Furnace
207 Stringed Instrument Collection
208 Buying the Painted Turtle

PINION (2002)

211 Asunder
213 Curing Time (Preacher)
214 The Proof-Meter
215 Pinion
217 Fine as Silk
218 Her Heart's Cream
220 The Admirer
222 Bathing Mother
223 Threshold
225 Baiting the Trap
226 Caul
226 Hoarfrost
227 Curing Time (Sister)
229 Glove
231 The Deer
232 Snowbound, Christmas

PHARAOH, PHARAOH (1997)

235 Searching the Title
237 Auction
238 Airstream
241 Portrait
242 The Milk Cow Speaks of Winter
243 The Moon Is Made
244 In the Acoustic Shadow
245 Skin Deep
247 Prodigal
249 Plagues
251 Transgressions
254 Barn Cat
255 Gossip
257 Stoic
258 Phoenix

259 *Afterword*, by Dave Smith
261 *Notes*

ungrafted
new poems

CISTERN

The place leased for pasture, cows roam what
was the yard, the garden, arbor grazing close
to the house—doorless, windowless—filled upstairs
and down with hay. Their bodies the color
of weathered marble, created light, muscle
makes fluid allusion to bone as they lower
their heads to drink, their breath causing the cistern's
moon to quake as they fade into each
other, museful ghosts, both form and void.

SINGLE SHOT

I cannot recall what birthday it was,
my ninth or twelfth, when my parents gave me

a single-shot .22—and a sewing machine.
The machine was unwrapped, only a pretty bow

on the top of its shiny new cabinet,
purposeless to me as a casket. The rifle

they swaddled in shimmering paper, gave it
a matching bow at the end—what I knew

Was a barrel. I had asked for neither.

My father never killed anything I knew about,
and still he kept what had been given to him

as a boy—a shotgun, a rifle or two, all bundled
tight as the old, their thin bodies in thick

bed quilts stored underneath the bed. He taught me
to shoot the way he taught me to swim,

to read, to recite verses from the Bible.

The husband of my youth ate no meat
for twenty years and still he kept loaded

guns leaning in the corners. *You never know,*
he said. Once he had just gotten out of the shower

and noticed a skunk stumbling into the yard
in full daylight; declaring it rabid, he grabbed

the shotgun, ran naked into the yard to shoot it.
How we laughed at that. When he was drunk,

and there was nothing else, he shot up the sky.

WOMAN HUMMING

Spring, and a woman sees in the paper
that a bear has entered the city,

having come impossibly down to it,
following the narrowed,

wild margin along the river, its rock cliffs
and berries the perfect

seduction of one awakened from a long
night of ice, where she starved

even in dream. Almost old, the woman keeps
to herself on her

front porch, her voice not quite a sigh, not crying,
hers a sing-song-yawn,

the kind of nothing a woman hums
to a placid infant,

comforting herself. Childless, never
married, widow-like

her presence, she rocks in her chair, ignored
by neighbor-boys, never

still, who will soon spend the summer on scooters,
skates—those grating blades—

on the sidewalk in front of her house. She knows
the bear would have gone

under the interstate, its passover
so high she must have

mistaken it for dry thunder, pleasing
sky-sound, familiar

as the rush the river makes. And then she knows—
because she has seen it—

the fences shorten and turn, the stones becoming
one—white and flat—and a black

path of asphalt unrolls as though from a bolt.
She must have followed

that pitted ribbon of earth raveling to this
inescapable:

A cat, an old tom with a milky eye, eats
whatever she is eating

from her hand, while the boys are wild with waiting
on the corner for the bus

that will, for a little while longer, take them up
from the rest of her life.

LOW SUNDAY

The week before, the sanctuary had been
overfull, children restless in new linen,
lilies overwhelming the already close,
humid air, even the balcony so crowded
that by the second hymn they fanned themselves
with their bulletins.
                                        Attendance this morning,
though—predictably poor, and in the collection
plates, the slimmest few coins. He had prepared
communion himself, thimbles of what passes
for wine, for blood, he poured down the drain.
But the bread, severed into perfect cubes, dice-sized,
he throws out for sparrows in the churchyard,
and they fall on it, delighted as though
for the first time with his most predictable
of miracles, having again paid no
attention to the hand that has performed it.

FACE BLINDNESS

She wants the eggs so she can hollow them,
And she keeps chickens

In the pen where the goats were until someone
Came and took them away.

But there is an ordinance against this too
And the neighbors who remain

Strangers complain until she brings the hens
Into the house, to save them,

Eats her supper sometimes with one of them
In her lap. They nest

In the back of the piano, in the cradle.
She goes out to gather

Cicadas for them to eat, the plague of one
Summer a bounty,

A legion of wings; she takes a bucket the way
She would to gather

Raspberries that ripen along the river.
How carefully she harvests them,

Looking down along the street for glassine
Wings, the panes' thin leading.

She paints the face of no one she knows on the canvas
Shells, her strokes careful,

Capillary thin, her brushes sharp
As needles, sharp as the scritch

Of their feet strolling across the floor, the sky lost
To them, the silent cicadas,

This otherworldliness closer to the faceless sun.

RED SAM IN THE DAYS THAT FOLLOW

"But nobody's killed," June Star said with disappointment . . .

And so, after the news that they are dead,
murdered, the lot of them, even the baby,
he relishes telling anyone who will listen
how he was the last to see them alive,
how he served them their last meal, how
the old woman had pretended to dance,
sitting in that very chair, to the Tennessee Waltz,
a lady from the better times, that one—

but also, now, in the looking back, how the smart-
mouthed little girl had been mightily impressed
with herself. Yes, the world is early rid
of trouble there, he shakes his head as though
she is still tap-dancing in the middle of that very floor
a memorized routine even a monkey could learn.

EARLY ELEGY: THYROID

She doesn't need it, they say—no one does—
one morning pill its formulary twin—
chrysalis-like, synthetic measure of the heart,
heat, blood. On the desk, a plastic figure models
her small gland's shape and size—a butterfly's,
like the one resting at the base of her throat, wings open,
basking, for now, just above the sternum's notch,
the way it might above a drying puddle.

PLANER

The husband of my youth did not know
I had taken out

the dismemberment insurance—so much for a foot,
a leg, an arm, more for

the dominant side of anything. I got it
cheap through the JC Penny,

figuring it was better than the nothing
there would be otherwise.

Then once, by accident of course, he fed
his hand into the planer;

he said he was listening to "Rank Stranger"
in his headphones,

running boards for something he resented
having to build. When

the machine was on, he said the blades disappeared
into their own spun-motion,

the way he wished to, perhaps, and so he simply
let his eyes lie and reached in

for some reason he could not later recall.
He drew back a hand

with a finger gone at the first joint—lucky
the doctor would say,

reattaching the part we brought with us wrapped
in his handkerchief. I recall

the stitches, a ring of them black and tight—how
that finger never regained

its feeling, not fully, or so he said, how it felt
strange to him, a chill

so pale it might have belonged to someone else.
And it made me feel that much

worse—like keeping from him a secret
account, his piecemeal worth.

PITTY SING IN ARMS

Her son, Bailey, didn't like to arrive at a motel with a cat.

And so, the womb of your basket is
forgotten, and the sound of the engine
beneath the floor replaced by wind soughing
through the branches of a pine. This time
there is nothing left to do but climb
the tree you find yourself thrown against.
So—after going high as the branches allow,
all the while the voices below dwindling

into the aftersound of sharper sounds—you begin
the slower climb back down to find and twine
yourself around the legs of a kinder man
who picks you up to run against a hand
as though familiar down your knowing spine,
then all along the length of your languid tail.

LUCYNELL IN HEAVEN

The body, lady, is like a house: it don't go anywhere, but the Spirit,
lady, is like a automobile: always on the move, Always . . .

And so, her cheek pressed warm against the curious
counter, she wakes to the word in which she has
delighted since he arrived and fixed it for her,
pretty in her mouth. She cannot see him
now, but on saying it again can
for the first time hear it—*burrttddt ddbirrrttdt*
no longer hers alone, but this other man's
who hears it, too, strokes her hair with one hand,

and with the other places before her a warm plate
of ham the red of a field newly turned and grits
white as the dense mist that was the field's, now lifted.
She hears music from the jukebox confusing itself with light
and sound, all of it the winged abandonment that is
song: here, eat, he says, angel *bird* of *Gawd.*

BUS IN THE QUARRY

1.

Down and down to the watery jaw
        of the earth they cut,
taking and taking until the absence

cratered, filled with this—refusal,
        or a forgetting—this
something with the countenance

of a pond, its sheeted rock walls
        bearing the silhouettes
of birds, the granite's glistening

reflection another cliff you can
        see through, odd clarity
for wild water—wind on the surface
        its only current.

2.

If you look long enough, you can
        make out a school bus
the men sunk years ago. On weekends,

they practice saving children, or,
        more likely, recovering
the bodies of the ones they won't save.

They strategize; they unwrap
        sandwiches their wives
packed for them, suit up against

the cold and time under, swim
        into the bus's gutted
shell and out of its ghostly

windows. All day, then, they breathe
        under the water,
pretend this is a crisis.

3.

Every year or so, someone
        drowns in it—having
mistaken the calm, the seen-depth

for guilelessness. And for a while
        flowers appear at the cliff's
edge where some boy swung out and dropped

into his joyous scream—until
        his name disappears
from the roster, from the mouths of those

who called out for him that day,
        and the rope, still hanging
straight and still as a plumb rule—

beckons with spring, wisteria climbing
        with another one
who thinks to show them—just watch—
        how not to forget.

TEMPORARY MADNESS

Perhaps it was never hers to tell,
        with no one to tell it to.
And so it became this: The early

1930s and she was unmarried,
        in nursing school,
her uniform an apron like a butcher's,

long and white as at the bleached
        beginning of day,
or a curtain drawn at the end.

The rest of her wasted behind it;
        behind her the quickening,
her spine vulnerable as a sapling,

and as willful. Perhaps she was
        trying to give it back
when she threw it down the hospital's

elevator shaft, determined
        to return somehow what
cannot be returned, the bell's toll,

sworn oath, curse hurled into the eye of a well—
        that hollow column,
dry oblivion catching the backward born.

Temporary madness was the diagnosis,
        and with it, the kind
of forgiveness that must have been

its own damnation, severest mercy,
        every other child
she bore its voice—that healthy a cry,
        inconsolably so.

JOY IN THE LOFT

Whenever she looked at Joy this way, she could not help but feel that it would have been better if the child had not taken the Ph.D.

And so, it is not only the leg, taken
this second time, she laments, but the eye, the one
she imagines in the valise in the hollowed-out
Bible, socketless eye for the eye lost
as the leg as it had been hers, a dimly remembered
girl's. She doesn't need to look down, through
the nothing in which she is professed to believe,
but she does, of course, willing the body again

toward it, invisibility, pure space.
The blind brain arguing with the mind even now,
the missing arch tingles as though waking
from sleep as the calf muscle tenses,
quiet, rebellious, from climbing
the ladder to this: phantasm-what-is.

LEARNING TO DIVE

Enthralled all afternoon with myself, I was
        Intent on learning how

To form my body, train it to follow my hands
        Like the apex of a triangle

So I would plunge sharp, clean—head, spine,
        Hips, legs following in an arc,

Feet neatly paired, pointed. I imagined
        Myself a bow, a blade

Of flexed tempered steel—or water pouring
        From an invisible pitcher, returning

To itself. And once in the water, I exhaled
        Slowly, opened my arms

To reverse my descent, water murmurous
        In my ears. I had not thought

Much about the lake, common to me
        As elementary school, church, something

I had never not known. I could not
        Remember learning to swim there,

In water tea-like, warm enough to dissolve
        Sugar, floating dock a tethered planet

Of rough boards. But as I waited my last turn,
        Watching the others disappear one

By one into the reflection of a late
        Afternoon sky, I considered how this

Lake had been a creek, had run through farms,
    The men had dammed it, water

Sank an old house not worth moving, fields
    Of tobacco, good pastureland.

At what depth, I wondered, my few years—
    For roots to rot, shifting silt

Settle, thicken, grow its own plants, water's
    Fields that needed no light. My turn

Came, I hesitated, my invincibility
    Already a remembered thing, but

Dived again, seeking the form mine,
    Imperfect, there, but shaping itself.

JAGUAR

This was what we first feared, then coveted,
and knew we could never achieve—densely
fleet night-climber, swimmer, its leap one of mute
beauty into flight. So we fashioned a likeness
of glossed gold to wear jewel-like, the hollowed
lightness of its body a chamber for the stone
we placed inside—a percussive pulse we made
obedient to the poverty of our bodies,

the fire we circled suddenly finer-muscled,
the shadows we cast leaping higher than we could,
the figment of all desire we bound to us,
green-eyed at the waist, across the chest—fire-glozed—
its soul that small stone, lonely bone, such bright-
quickening we could believe to be our own.

BACHELOR-BROTHER

He spends the days teaching someone's indifferent
children what he has accepted to be
the withered art of declension, grammar, meaning
itself; evenings, of late, alone and childless,
he takes up the known dead he suspects will be
his only survival, their similar indifference
to him aside. He has mined a bloodline
generations deep, looking for provenance—
or cause, his computer screen a ledger filled
with abstracts, diplomas, certificates
of birth, death, schedules of mortality,
cemetery records, census after
census, now and again a face in a photograph
the size of a postage-stamp.
                                        When this wearies him,
he transfigures that same screen into some
semblance of the living—purchases time
with bath-house steam, the naked anonymous
small as the palm of his hand. He prefers this
to the town's married men he will not risk
settling for, invites in—"oh"—he says,
the stories he does not tell.
                                        His rooms
dim, curtained, on his bedroom wall
he has hung a mosaic of old mirrors,
an eclectic display he has made to behave
like a church's clerestory, too high
to see into, so that he can believe,
sometimes, they are windows he sleeps beneath,
and the silvered light that falls from them
onto his bed not relative, but true.

HERE NOR THERE: PARTICIPANT OBSERVATIONS

The B_______s are all slew-footed and slow; they
walk like they're plowing behind a mule, the kind

of slew a corrective brace does not help; they
just go right back to the way God made them. Case

in point Uncle D_______, slew-footed and bent over
at the waist like a hinge frozen at the partial. And he

walked with his hands clasped behind his back, like
he was deep in thought instead of trying to keep

his knuckles from dragging the sidewalk. He couldn't read
his own name but walked that way to town every day

to get the paper so Aunt S_______ could read it out loud
to him. She lost both her legs to the sugar diabetes.

When they buried her it was in a child-size casket, cheaper
and frilly as a dollhouse. But that's neither here nor there.

The E_______s are all nervous; you can pick them out
at church just by the foot swinging and hand

wringing. They are good with ciphering and reading
out loud with expression. Nerves combined with

worry has made more than one of them good
accountants. Case in point Uncle C_______ who

learned to sell by selling radios
to folks who didn't have current yet.

One time he sold enough General Electric
refrigerators in a year to win a trip

all the way to Germany and he went on a boat
down the Rhine and left his whole family at home.

He brought his wife a china tea set she has
never once used. But that's neither here nor there.

DEGREES OF RAPE

I have been worried again about
        the degrees of rape,
about what counts these days and what

does not, what men call legitimate,
        meaning aggravated
and violent, and what they say

is easy—illegitimate, then.
        I was nineteen, dancing
right in front of the band; my peasant blouse's

intricate stitching bright green
        and yellow I recall
admiring in the ladies' bathroom

mirror, and also the way my nipples
        showed through sheer cotton.
It has always been easy to tell

myself I must have wanted it,
        to swallow that night,
to take all of it in and keep it,

not to breathe, then or now, the back
        of my throat still, sometimes—
this day—that strangled place. I must have

asked for all of it—they would say—
        the dance floor, the man
leaning into a microphone

who watched me twirl the way the mirror
        had watched me, the way
I turned and turned toward and then

away from him so he could admire
        the braids I had made
but could not see, long and heavy

coursing down my back even now.

THE BOOKMOBILE LADY

Pittsylvania County, Virginia

She said the first one was something like the truck
    that delivered milk to the folks in town. But women

drove it and women walked to meet it, time
    and place predetermined, a church's parking lot,

country store, a crossroads—never mind the mud,
    the dust, all of them home-bound, child-bound, crop-

bound. She ferried requests from the month before,
    some newer novels, mysteries, romances,

this a cargo meant for lending, not to be kept—
    and better than the way their houses would not

be kept, a book consumed the way the baking
    of a loaf of bread consumed the fire they set

and measured in the cook-stove, invisible such
    leavening, ancient, temporal. When a woman

signed the card to take a volume home,
    it was likely the one time she wrote her name

all month—wrote anything at all, her signature
    slim, unpracticed correspondence with the next

woman who would choose the same, and proof that she
    was here and would return, something she got to keep.

CONFESSION

Her preferred way of talking to me
is on the table, near at hand, like a card

played face up, the small screen a votive,
the letters she knows, rosary-like, her fingers

moving over them without thought. She
rummages in her gaping bag for the small plastic

sacks of green tea, organic rice she has brought—
fragrant remedies—all the while relishing

the recitation of her usual
complaints, that pressure behind her eyes, that

ringing in her ears. She finally produces
the paperback of diseases and causes

she wants me to read, turns to the page
she has marked, the why of my tumor

explained, the what, the could-be stress,
unhappiness, a secret, see, some guilt

made manifest. She means well, I mean
to tell myself, while I confess instead

what I want to say to her, her ear
a fertile, pearled receptacle: *Listen:*

I want to tell it to you; I want to
let you have it, hut it up in you,

so at last there will be something about you
I do not, and can never know.

CRAWL SPACE

The ache in the widow's hip its own divining,
the radio crackling

with it, she tries to believe it's imagined,
part of the storm gathering—

that crying wafting up from the crawl space.
Her neighbor reminds her

of her younger self, and so she relishes
telling her a thing

or two, some kind of mean relief in sending her
through the foundation's

small door, the one she never locks, herself
somehow beneath her feet,

the house heavy above her. She can imagine
bellying past flowerpots

near the door where she put them. Through
abandoned webs, into

the shadowy underside of the porch,
then back farther beneath

the kitchen, such close space good for little,
the kind of place things go

to die, and there finding them, not much
of a litter, two kittens,

scrawny, birth-blind. She will bring them out,
and the widow will give them

water from an eyedropper and swaddle them
in one of her old sweaters.

They accept it all as she must, given what
she knows the wind can seem.

L'INCONNUE DE LA SEINE

I saved her many times when I was a girl
        her age, my mouth on her mouth, my breath
                in her lungs, her chest rising with the measure

I was to learn from her. She had been brought out
        of a distant river I would never see
                or swim, the smile on her face not that of the drowned

but of the serene, a secret made immortal
        behind the mask of wax. I would have a whistle
                around my neck, and a cross stitched to my suit

at the hip. I would be given other children
        to watch over, knowing what little I knew
                from her, the one I thought I would survive.

A MOTHER'S DAY POEM FOR MARY, MOTHER OF GEORGE

We gather here where she prayed
for her son at war,

as mothers still pray for their children,
for the end of other wars.

Perhaps she could sense that the children's
voices of the next

century and the century after it
would rise God-like as though

in endless answer to her, to this
worn outcrop of stone.

Hers has long been a vulnerable
peace, a place that could be

bought and sold, deeded, re-deeded,
before history would make

its finer claim on her. This fence
and gate of wrought iron

must remind us that there is no mourning,
no elegy that does not

celebrate, that does not recall
our own mothers, all nascent

thought prayer-like, wordless quickening—
the voice we heard first

and believed to be our own, we hallow
with hers, indivisible from it.

ESCHATOLOGIES

Hothouse flowers
        someone brings
                tulips   out of season

in a sleeve
        of plastic   a tent
                where they cannot breathe

and still I cannot bear
        to unbind them   water them
                I let them live like that

for a day or so before
        I cast them swaddled
                into the trash

so remote are they are
        from   the comfort
                she thought to mean

for me, gave instead
        to herself   pristine
                this opposite

I am in love
        with the sounds
                of the people

below my room
        this small balcony
                anonymous bed

purchased I hear
        a fork on porcelain
                laughter the in-crowd

I overhear
   a live recording   I'm in with it.

basil bolts   while I am
away   bees become the weight

metronomic the sway
drunken almost

sweet largo a-spray

glass the sound
substance reflective,

transparent ice breaking,
a bottle, a window through

which a bird flies
luckless makes the house

I have my head in the tube, the can, and it is tight against my face my friend who had great Sorrow used to tell a story about her drunken father, how he would empty a can down to the dregs of tuna fish and leave it by the bank of the shallow pond until one of the feral cats would be made bold enough by hunger to stick its head into the dark opening. He would shoot it, then, in the head, and laugh at the implosion, the body convulsive left out for the world to watch the way my body is left out.

A PASTORAL

for Nicola and Bix

She has made for us a table of doors—
	Knobless, hingeless—covered
With bedsheets. Candlelit the room,

Its flaws the light makes lovely for this
	Asylum from a cold
Spring evening. Her daughter's dollhouse

Seems as real, its rooms open
	To the same light and warmth.
She tells us over mismatched bowls

Of steaming soup about her work—
	The rescue of bees,
Hives that have taken their own asylum

In the rot of these old houses, soffits
	And eaves, hollow columns
A favorite, she says, something

About the long and narrow, the strictness
	Of the space. But they are
Almost all sick, she says; her own hive

She had kept in a house the size
	Of the one for dolls
And tended—the way God would if

God had a more nimble hand—did not
	Survive the winter,
All of the bees dead as of a week ago,

As though a small planet's gravity
	Had suddenly failed.
Every once in a while there is

The rising pitch of wine filling
        A glass, then the bottle
Resettling on the table. Our spoons

pass again, again into emptying
        bowls; the candles gutter,
shuddering the sheets; her child
        cries for her bed.

UNGRAFTED: JEFFERSON'S VINES

You might have considered the root that resisted
drought sand mold, that its blander grape would be
better sacrificed to the vine with the fickle bloom,
but a sweeter yield. Not quite invention that would have been,
the manipulation of the garden; if such is flesh
you would have considered it nonsensical
to the severance. And that would have become the bottle.
What you might have made the candle-flame entered anyway,

the real quickening, evening a slip like a blade
into it. As a dream inheres even into afternoon—
of it, and other—as it dissolves like salt
in broth, like light in water, that was the graft
of what you did with what you might have done—
what might have become the tongue, becoming it.

claude before time and space
(2018)

SWIMMING ALONE

for Ann Dickinson Beal

A half mile
        down the dirt road
                to the house it passes

where an old woman lived
        until she died there,
                the rooms still

comfortable in their cool
        emptiness; then, a half mile
                farther past her, the farm pond

we find as empty. The widow
        was the one who told us
                not to be afraid

        to do it, to swim
                there alone. She said
                        she had long ago

formed the habit
        of this water's solitude,
                the habit of this
                        afternoon, all the late

afternoons conspiring
        to one: not exactly
                swimming, the way

we suspend
        ourselves in water,
                two old friends

who would say
we are living alone,
divorced and listless in it,

in letting ourselves drift
on what little current
survives the damming,

the push and pull
of the small creek
that feeds this, makes it.

The water's
temperature is of nothing,
of the womb.

We love it that
we can't feel it
as anything as apart

from us. We never
fail to speak of it. And
never fail to fall quiet

enough for the beaver,
near-blind, to swim
so close to us

we can feel its wake,
hear the fat slap of the tail.
There is the smell

of a hot innertube
where dragonflies find us,
the blue of a widow skimmer

net-veined that lights
on my island-hand,
its body broken

into syllables.
Algae blooms unbroken,
a green roil,

thunder moseying
around the hem of the water,
and I have become unafraid

even of lightning strikes.
So when, now, this
afternoon years impossibly

past, I learn she is dying,
there is selfish comfort
in knowing she is doing this

thing before me, the way
she is in the middle
of the pond before I

can get there, not facing the dock,
not waiting for me,
but away, considering

the other bank, a turtle
dozing on a log,
the catfish visible

beneath the log, a snake's
head threading the air
above its body.

She is unafraid as I
would have been afraid if I had
arrived before her, too timid

to leave the heat-
splintered dock. If she is able
to imagine a place,

I imagine this is hers.
And this poem is
not between us, not

yet imagined, the living
we have yet to do
there in its place. And

the swallows have yet
to give up the sky
to the bats,

and the bullfrogs
have yet to begin
what passes for song,

for descant, and the shy green
herons have yet
to return to their nests.

We have to wait
for the new moon to rise,
red and thin as a bass's
gill, clean and bloodless,

through which we have
to learn
to breathe again.

THE WHEEL

Once a year, the carnival people would travel
the county schools and give out free tickets
to us children—wheedling power at home.

And so my father would end up in the bingo tent,
placing dried pinto beans on tired numbers,
winning the free game, a chance at something,

while my mother, joyless, patient, would watch me,
her purse clutched tight against strangers, evening
itself. Here, there were the usual gilts

and shoats, ribboned hogs, calves; I recall a ring
in the nose of a bull: creatures we would slaughter
later and talk over at the table, those ribbons

forgotten in a drawer. But the clowns
were there, the concessions, the smell of burned
sugar, seared salt, and we were there beneath

painted lights, a confusion of sound—
canned song and the screams of country children
taught silence—made briefly bold with the artifice

of joy. The carousel I refused, and the tired
ponies in their dusty ring of misery.
Everything else, the scrambler, the roller coaster

that hurtled my brother through the air—too dangerous,
too loud—the ferris wheel was the one something
my mother and I could agree on, and so

I would concede to choose it, the up and over
physics that no longer thrilled anyone.
I could already understand the ease of it,

the predictable safety in something
made with the same materials as the simplest
bridge we had crossed to get here: steel, iron

rivets, the easy welds, girders, bolts, and cables,
the soul of a pinion gear the axis—
built with the same tools, same labor, the industry

the same. The sweating huckster would let me
ride longer, no one in line for the spine made circle,
its bent taken to extreme: its span time—

not distance—bridging nothing much, this day
with the next, this hour the arc. My ticket
had been free, to see what I always saw—

but aslant—from the bright gondola's cradle-sway—
the same fields, fenced horizon line, stalks of corn
and wheat, tobacco, soybeans, closer and farther,

to feel the breeze that came along the river, the breeze
the wheel made itself, the carnival rising
and falling that would be gone in the morning.

Motion's old architecture, this tired amusement,
nothing to break, nothing to ruin, little
to fail it but my attention—that turning

in my gut gravity, like love, immortal,
if weary, and what the wheel lifted me through,
stately and serene, it would resist

with the same resolve in ferrying me back down.

PRE-ALGEBRA, 1970

for Dr. Maria Dolores Choca

That she had earned a PhD
        in mathematics
                at Universidad de La Habana

was not part of what she told
        the Pre-Algebra
                eighth grade, crowded

into an airless trailer-classroom
        tucked behind
                the high school—afterthoughts,

the lot of us, already taller
        than she was,
                some stinking of woodsmoke,

some with mud on our shoes.
        We figured out
                soon enough, though,

the one question that would
        free us from her
                ceaseless attempts

to convince us that algebra
        was the same
                as bone-setting,

the missing with what
        was missing, the like
                with the like. So

we would beg her
        to tell us about the night
                she escaped Castro,

and she would—on her
gesturing arm the smallpox
vaccine scar the size

of a half-dollar, moon-
cratered—pointing every time
at us as though

we were no longer
there—telling again and again
about leaving with nothing,

the smell of rubber
and gasoline, the engine cut,
swimming all night, breathing

inside a hissing vortex
of water and salt,
swallowing her screams

like ground glass. We
had never seen the ocean
she swam to get to us,

had heard little other
than the familiar thickness
of our own accents—

but by spring, despite
ourselves, we knew it all,
every word, well

enough to perform
for each other even the required
lapses, laughing, into Spanish.

And beyond the narrow
        classroom window, the field
                of broomsedge and sumac

we had paid such hard-
        blind attention to
                had turned into something

we no longer quite
        saw, or tried to see past,
                and that would be our

inescapable—
        and most boring
                of mistakes,

the like with the like.

A LIFE BEYOND

for Maurice Manning

You have told me
    you passed into the space
        beneath the loft,

the hayhook,
    and, as though from
        a darkened theatre,

looked out through
    the opposite door
        into 1880, the cicadas

the same, you could hear,
    the light changed somehow
        but how you cannot say.

Your great-grandmother is
    the girl in the field,
        grasses to her

collarbone. She has no doll,
    yet, not even that
        pretense of the you

she will never know.
    She has slipped away
        from the house, from

some small task
    she has been assigned,
        something with the dullness

of a spoon and bowl,
    perhaps—just to turn herself
        around out there,

in the sun, having spun
        through the shadows
                of the animals, having

turned herself inside
        their breathing. That is
                your crooked land,

exactly; you have seen
        your name
                on the deed. You are

in the cleft of her chin,
        the brow bone, in
                a face she has begun

to admire when she makes
        a ladle of her hand,
                and brings it to her

mouth to drink. She
        does not know
                that she has disappeared,

or that someone
        will be looking
                for her. She should

not be alone—
        at the spring, in this
                field—and so she is not.

ON LEAVING THE BODY TO SCIENCE

The *my* becomes
a *the*, becomes
the state's

the coroner's,
something
assignable,

by me, alone,
though it will not
be the *I*

I am on
leaving it, no
longer to be

designated human or
corpse: *cadaver*
it will be,

nameless patient
stored in
the deep hold

of the hospital
as in the storage
of a ghost ship

run aground—
the secret in it
that will,

perhaps, stir again
the wind that
failed. It

will be pickled,
        kept like larva,
                like a bullet

sealed gleaming
        in its chamber.
                They will gather

around it,
        probe and sample,
                argue—then

return it
        to its between-
                world, remove

their aprons
        and gloves
                and stroll, some evenings,

a city block
        for a beer,
                a glass of chilled

white wine. Even there, they
        will continue
                to speak of it,

what they
        glean from beneath
                the narrative

of scars, surgical
        cavities, the
                wondrous

mess it became
    before I left it
        to them

with what's
    left of me, this
        name, a signature,

a neatened
    suture, perfect, this
        last, selfish stitch.

MIDWIFE

all the women pregnant   it seems
        to me   in a hollowed out
shadow carved   Tennessee farmland

hippie buses and vans   our hair
        in long braids   feathers
woven into them   and we all

resist white fluorescence
        sterile forceps   needles
so I decide to learn it

myself   and I do   read
        old texts   study grainy
photographs   mostly the babies

come out all right   on their own
        until I have guided thousands
into these   close rooms   windows

open to summer   or open
        to winter   to cicadas
or snow   a sameness to it

after all   the crowning   glistening
        whorl of hair   beneath
the fontanelle   iridescent

pulse   a well-eye
        one that will close   that is
already closing   over   time

I see the rarer cord-
        strangled   ones too early
or too late   hidden twins

ones who come fists first
breeches   stills   but there is
the one   singular   one

born in the bread truck
his parents have driven
there   they are living in it

broken down   beside
a foundation   they are
digging   out of mud   when I arrive

he is already coming   I see
first his mouth   so like his
mother's sucking before

he breathes   the rest of the head
appears   I see   no skull
just the brain   exposed

before the rush   of the rest
of him   perfect   I have read
about it   this thing the book's

glossary defines as   *monster:*
mutation   saltation   freak
so I take him from her

he breathes on his own   I let him
he does not laugh
or cry   for the one month he lives

though he does make a sound
otherworldly   and after
he dies   only after   do the other

infants in the barn-like nursery
        make it   for a while   echoing
something not quite language   not quite

song   un-syllabled that vowel   that
        does not rise or fall, bottomless
in that way,   and what they

have learned from him is as though
        from some place beyond
that only he among them   could recall

become in the raw wake of him
        something they must remember
and   will in the telling

and retelling   they are   I am
        for a while   now
sure   this   sure of it

RABBIT

1.

Same as you, Claude says, creature of habit,
travelling the same narrow path worn
slick, through broomsedge and scrub pines.

To hear him tell it, the hotel in town
still stands, wants to buy every rabbit
you have for a quarter a piece, the meat

lean and dark, cleaned and ready to be
cut up for the frying pan. So you fashion

a trap—you'll need 10 of them for 50
acres from whatever scraps of wood
and wire you can scrounge from around

the place—and nail it long and narrow, set it
to face the path. Same as you—for an apple
core—same as you, he'll come around.

2.

You go around with a lantern every
morning before light; right away you
know you've got one by the little door

being shut. You reach in and grab it quick
by the hind legs; that's where the strength is.
You know the way you would a newborn

to smack it alive? Hold it tight and upside down.
Sometimes one dies from the fear, saving you

the trouble, but in any case, all it
ever takes is this—quickest clip with the edge
of your hand, see, right here behind the neck.

You can skin it easy with your fingers;
it's slick—he leans over, slips the sock off
your foot—as this.

RABIES

Claude says beware when creatures lose their fear
of you, of daylight—become afraid instead
of water, even in hottest July. You cannot

trust what looks like taming, the skunk ambling
into the dooryard, fox slowed, a torporous
emergence from the trees, from the thorn-etched

bracken as though saved, answering God's
call, or yours. Unmistakable,

the transfiguration you must destroy,
the single shot to the head, the severing of it
to send the skull—its brain—in a sack

to Richmond for the accounting, to prove
what you already know. The rest of it, though,
you are to burn at home in the barrel with the trash.

DRYBRIDGE

1.

Claude says he, too, was given the tracks and not
the train, the way—and not the way out, not the beyond
beyond that bend, or the next. The place

they call Drybridge—for the waterless bed
of rails—where on the banks, you grow up learning
more news from hoboes than from the mailman.

But you know nothing of the train as it passes
behind the backs of grander houses, gutted

warehouses, chained dogs, as it grazes an alien
grid of fences—of stone, metal, and chainlink.
Or that when it passes beneath the underside

of a bridge, a boy your own age waves the way
you do, and that there is a horse doesn't lift its head,
and one that does, only to lower it again.

2.

You are a grown man when the train comes
to a scalding stop, and a lantern swings down
the road. A man has been killed, they call out

from behind the light, and would you come see
what you can tell of him by what's left. You do
know his hat, and that burn scar on the back

of his hand. What you know of his wife
you do not say and will not even the next

night when you sit up with the body in the house
he wanted that much shut of, her voice rigid
as its walls while the train you hear out there in the darkness

passes by the way it always does, as though
the same, the very same, and, again, on
the time it will this night be able to keep.

BEFORE SPACE

You crawl on top of what had been the field,
the summer; the leaves clouded in white cloth
beneath you, you think to sleep the night it takes

to get the tobacco crop to market, the wagon's
rumbling lessened by the load. You wake, though,
at the sound of your father's voice telling you to,

his arm out as though sighting something between
the mule's ears: What do you see? And you know

what it is, they are, the two beings spheres
of light at the horizon. So you say it:
two moons, and he laughs that you could easier

imagine that than an automobile's headlamps.
It still makes for a better answer, Claude says,
the heavens transfigured in that one night

or that you could imagine such a thing.
And now it is not the stuff of your imagination,
or the television screen, this thing they have

named everyone's comet, though you call it
yours because it is so close that you
don't need even binoculars to see it,

to notice its long hair streaming behind it
as though windblown, or gravity-blown, something

falling though it is not, something on fire
you would have said had your father set this
instead in the sights between the mule's ears,

because you had seen what can happen when you
lean in too close. And your naked eye
is enough as it has to be when you stay up

all night at the tobacco barn, where you are
to feed small fires in the ovens made
from mud and dust like daubers' nests, from where

you can see no other light beyond those
small needy ones that are not fixed part of the patterned
sky, unlike this bright body so new

to you, moving low against the same horizon.
It is enough to love the world again, the heavens

changed—and not by something with a flameless tail
of gasses and dust, they say, its core a nucleus
of ice—but by what you would have said and still

think when you watch for it of an evening,
this late, unmistakable surprise: a woman's
face. Gravity's fire. See how she leans in to you.

the opposite house

(2015)

HOUSE SPARROWS

They are here, in the eaves, the clothesline pole,
hayloft—everywhere she looks—and everywhere
she goes they are there before her, in town,
in streetlamps, hooded stoplights, in letters
at the pharmacy, cursive, neon serifs.
She knows they prefer human-made hollows,
though she finds them also in the branches
of evergreens and hawthorns. She entices
the nieces and nephews, whom she dislikes
in equal measure, with a Sunday afternoon's
escape from themselves, and so they learn
to follow her while she spots a nest, then
knocks it down with the longest pole on the place.
They race to the small-domed thing to break it
open like a present, unwrap outer
layers of twigs and roots, tear past the middle
membrane of woven grass, sometimes scraps
of cloth, to find the warm, innermost lining
of feathers. If there is a clutch of eggs
speckled bluish-white, they have learned
to throw them against the barn's wall,
where they explode into a constellation
of watery stars.
                                        If there are hatchlings,
the children, delighted, toss them, one after
the other, into the chicken yard—where
she has despised most of all the bold greed
with which the birds steal feed. The chickens,
who have never minded sparrows, fight
each other for every tender-boned, sweet
scream of rarest meat fallen into the lot
they will return to keeping grassless
as a cemetery swept clean of grief.

CLEARCUT

A Wounded Deer—leaps highest—
—EMILY DICKINSON

Her body is already harvested
of its children, its quickness, both breasts, its work,
most worry, all regret, the intervale
of sorrow behind her now. They planted
the loblollies for this, the old age they had
faith in, hers alone. Neighbors despair
that she would make wasted acres where
those trees had stood for so long they believed them
ownerless given. But if let be, they would
sicken and fail, he had said, all at one,
slowed once.
And so the men begin cutting,
inescapable the sound of chainsaw
cough and stutter, the felling, men calling out
to one another as though desperate
for something, the drag of chained logs through mud,
engines downshifting for days, weeks,
the stench of resin, gas, sawdust, oil,
exhaust. Then, the controlled burn, smoke fog-close
to the ground, wafting toward and then away from
the house, before the quiet of replanting
seedlings, trees she does not bother to
imagine.
Deer return to the yard, preferring
apples still hanging over those easier
fallen in the shadowy grasses; she watches
a doe's slow rise on hind legs as though in a freezing
leap, not of the wounded but of the resolved,
in its mouth what looks like a small sphere
of sweetest ice. Beyond it, she is able
to take in the main road, a broader swath
of sky, a mile of air—that much clarity.

SCARECROW AT THE FORKS OF BUFFALO

Late afternoon and the house is shut up
tight against night, the thready stream of smoke
that of a lesser fire, early-banked.
The husband, then, must be dead, or so long
gone she does not despair, the scarecrow
wearing his hunting jacket and watch cap,
red-blaze the only color that will burn
through the hour. Beneath the jacket, the figure
wears one of her nightgowns, sleep-thinned—or
sheer from sleeplessness, and still she could not
bear to throw it out farther than this
rough form from which she hung pie pans
one morning, shying in the breeze. Like scales
of some failed justice, they balance now
above the frozen plot, above the crows
that have lost all caution, the sound their wings
make near-vowel as they fly low to land
in ice-choked rows, to peck at hoarfrost,
frozen mud.
                    She is in bed but wakeful,
listening, not to crows, but to the faint fork
of the creek winter narrowed but quickened,
and the fainter but fevered keening of dogs
somewhere, scent-pitched, bodiless as though distance
itself had a voice and desire—the garden a seed
catalog, open on the kitchen table, that
one light she left on downstairs fixed on it.

CHARTING THE PARTICULARS

He reads it every morning. Like a mapmaker,
he must plot extremes before he can focus
on details, and the extreme of every day
is that the leg is gone, stubborn surprise
because the brain has never accepted it
and still sends down the most ludicrous
of commands, an itch on the missing shin, tickle
on the arch of a foot gone fifty years. Details
come down to rash, pinch, bruise, any flaw that might
prevent him from wearing the thing that leans
in the corner by the bed, ready before him,
in yesterday's sock and shoe, knee locked, bucket
yawning like the mouth of a catfish, landed
and gaping. Some days, in charting the particulars,
it reminds him of one of his children newborn,
before he had reason to dislike it.

He knew,
of course, that it was his, but found it alien
anyway—small, pale, hairless as this
small thing made hairless and pale. And he held it
the way he holds this now, at arm's length, gently
in his two hands, finding nothing familiar
at all, touching it, tenderly, this same way.

THIRD

He survived the first beach landing and an entire
world war for this: the textile mill, buildings
looming over the river, windows painted
black during the war so they could run the third
shift he came to choose—easier he found
to black out the days, shutter them, so that the hours
that had been for drinking or the dreams
he could better sleep through, to wake evenings
for cigarettes and coffee. The trick—not to wake
too much, avoid the gaze of the face in the mirror
as he shaved it, watch static on the television screen
or the crosshairs of a test pattern. Nights were
easier bright and loud—rooms the size
of airplane hangars, close as circus tents,
dye room, spinning room, his the weave room,
voiceless, lit with sound, rows of looms,
their ceaseless weft and warp, shuttles swift,
percussive—clawhammer-like—air thick
with the smell of cotton, lint in their lungs, their hair,
sheeting like dyed, transfigured fields, or fields
bleached to blinding, a collective shroud.
                                                            Graveyard shift
made them all equal, orphaned; those with families
saw them Sundays, afternoon its own ghost.
It was easier to bear what no one else wanted—
a world just lightening when his shift ended, the river
they all crossed running with the night's dye.

ENTRANCE

1.

Some evenings her own house convinces her
she is already dead, photographs framed
portals into which she sometimes falls
awake in another room. The phone is silent
in its cradle, food tasteless, even salt dumb
grains of glass. She calls someone who does answer
but a voice cannot convince her otherwise,
the self dead who called another woman's
husband with an innocent question the excuse
to hear his voice, the self who would have had
a cigarette about now, the lighter in a drawer
here somewhere, her initials engraved, a flourish
of cursive. She craved the sound of the thumbwheel's
scrape against flint, small flame, that first long drag,
the practiced rings of smoke she formed with a mouth
painted to disappear behind them. The glass
of driest sherry cannot persuade her, though
she drinks it anyway. Her hair, her fingernails,
her nakedness against the naked floor, the body
unbathed for days, some days, not enough.

2.

Too small to see into the upper nests,
she feels the sleeve of its body well muscled
with eggs. She knows her mother's fury
will be not only at the eggs lost,
but at the setting egg devoured also,
a doorknob of oblong, crazed porcelain
meant to trick the hens into laying.
She would have tried to kill the snake anyway,
but now has to be more certain of it,

lifting out the stuporous body
and quickly, deftly, severing the head,
offensive mouth with a paring knife
the way she has been taught. She massages out
a fluid wasteful braid of whites and yolks
shell-specked—what would have been more than enough,
she thinks, for a pound cake—before the knob
at last falls with a thud, like anything
but an egg, to the ground: small insistent
entrance to another house, any house,
a painted door, and, all to herself, one fool room.

CURSIVE

Children train instead the small muscles
in their hands to strike—uniform, precise—
preformed fonts of their choice. Frail evidence
of ornamental scripts (and cloven nibs, hairline
serifs), the signature, still required, survives,
though poorly executed, its likely demise
the scan of a single fingertip—loops, inkless
whorls—one, incorruptible exemplar.

SMALLPOX

The world has certified itself rid of
all but the argument: to eradicate or not
the small stock of *variola* frozen,
quarantined—a dormancy it has
refused, just once, for a woman behind a sterile
lens, her glass slide a clearest, most
becoming pane. How could it resist slipping
away with her, that discrete first pock?

LOCK

After the Emily Dickinson traveling exhibit at the Folger Shakespeare Library, Washington, D.C., 12 April 2012

> I noticed the quick wore off those things . . .
> —EMILY DICKINSON, ON DAGUERREOTYPES

The evening includes a reception, wine
and hors d'oeuvres with the curator, lighthearted
discussion of the various diagnoses,
hypotheses long debated—depression,
lesbianism, grief, agoraphobia,
the kind of anxiety a cat has
about the threshold, and the most recent
theory—epilepsy; that would explain it
all, they say, spasmodic punctuation,
reclusiveness, the shame, everything,
the hour of lead, at last, unlocked.
                                                  On display:
one of her beloved nephew Gilbert's
boyhood suits, velveteen, and beside it
the contents of his morning's pocket—a bullet's
spent casing, a wad of tangled string; drafts
of more famous poems bearing clearly
the needle-piercings where she sewed one
to another—the sutures of a fascicle's
finishing undone; what is thought to be
the only image ever made of her,
of which she disapproved, here, itself,
as yet without compare;
                                        and next to it,
the something rare, unexpected, lock
of her hair—the shape and circumference
reminiscent of a sparrow's nest, the color
she likened to a chestnut bur. She had brushed,
cut, coiled, and folded it into an envelope,

then sent it to someone, letter-like. Everyone
lines up to photograph it with their phones,
when what they must truly desire is to
touch it, as though they might feel the sheen
it retains. And while they can never
get close enough, they will never be any
closer than this to what it does not tell them,
and they are desperate for all that that might mean.

THE OPPOSITE HOUSE

This place:
a cavernous warehouse
of houses
dismantled,
cataloged,
reordered here
according
to part-rendered-
particle—
elemental—
the sentient
stuff of space
stored in meta-
space: this
room for doors,
thresholds,
staircases, risers
and stretchers,
banisters hand-
worn-smooth; this
for scrollwork,
moldings—egg
and tongue; for
floorboards—tongue
in groove; this
room for windows,
sills, sashes,
transoms; this
for mantles, shadow-
scents
of dead fires;
this a room
of bins: hinges,

doorknobs,
latches, locks. All
of it aged,
orphaned—
artifacts of the
slower fires
of neglect,
abandonment, before
bone-
pickers raced
the demolition for what
might be
salvaged to sell
again, like
prizing gold
from the teeth
of the dead, to be
re-measured, leveled,
grafted as though
re-made into
the agelessness
of someone else's
household-now.
As long
as they are
here, though, the fact
of every door
remains
reference to
an antecedent made
vague—a
cellar hole an
empty socket

somewhere, or
a sandy lot
opposite some
newer house,
a sidewalk's
stones' arrival
into grass,
or daffodils blooming
like wild,
unmeant things
in what
appears an old field
without design,
the kind
sumac prefers
and will
encircle—its
own transfiguring
salvage,
that—slow,
unambiguous.

RURAL LETTER CARRIER

For a brief while, the eighty-six miles gave some
illusion of travel, the seasons' slow
cycling part of it—the sky moving
from cloud to clearing, fields turned under
or crowded with corn, crows, soybeans, tobacco,
snow. But the road did not change, finally—
not the straight stretches, nor rain-fretted curves,
the relentless echo of gravel-ping, the hushing
of dust, mud-hiss and skunk-musk. The houses
went down over time, the men dying away,
then the widows; in the yards of emptied houses,
their children went on living in trailers with tires
on the roofs. And the names on the mailboxes
and the ones in the ragged graveyards were
the same. Some people hung their clothes from barbwire
fences to dry, and as long as I had been driving
that route delivering her check, one old woman
still hid behind the trunk of a sycamore
in her yard until I drove off again. Some days,
I stopped at the country store where a few bottles
of soda floated like blasted fish in the drinkbox,
where men checked deer and turkeys and bought bait,
where no one knew any news but of who died.
It only took my Sunday absence for a wren
or sparrow to begin a nest in a mailbox
forgotten open, or a hornet to finish one
that I'd find hanging down like a gray wattle
or venomous goiter from the throat.
They said there wouldn't be letters anymore,
what with people getting news through the air,
and money just numbers on a screen
that added up to a worse nothing, stored
in a machine somewhere—all of it invisible
and flying reckless, swarmless as thoughts

never meant to be spoken, then spoken.
I had driven through enough lonely
days to believe sometimes I passed by those hours
instead, like estranged houses to which I might
return some distant day, not to deliver
a day's worries and ordinary temptations—
but the letter addressed in a hand so far away,
so familiar, it would need no other understanding,
having found in me its last and only way.

COMMON HOUSE SPARROWS AT JFK'S INTERNATIONAL TERMINAL

They survive in factories, warehouses,
even coalmines; some were, after all, ship-borne,
and so that they are here should not surprise,
their small host a constant nervousness—
accepted, ignored—around and about
the food court's balcony, just above
security. From their perch—a skeletal
sculpture of abstracted aluminum
and guy-wire—they seek breadcrumbs, grains of rice,
of salt and sugar strewn beneath tables
and chairs, their survival dependent
on redundant carelessness.
                                        Perhaps they are not
captive here and meant to enter—through
an air vent or skylight; or, perhaps,
they succumbed to curiosity
and the happenstance of the automatic doors'
slow revolve to become the only natives
of this place, everyone else transient,
destinations ticketed, mirage-like.
They bask in what light manages to fall
through soot-fogged windows, or bathe in the slough
of neverending passage, arrivals
and departures in perfected synchrony—this
windless, rainless asylum sky enough.

VIRGINIA CHRISTIAN

The first female electrocuted in the state of Virginia in 1912, Virginia Christian was a 17-year-old African American maid who killed her white employer, the widow Ida Belote, after an argument that ensued when Belote accused Christian of stealing a locket. Belote's cruelty was well documented, and though Christian was a minor, the prosecution argued that her physical maturity have bearing on her sentencing.

A lynching gathering,
a horizon closing in,
the men
would hurry
to do it, send her
to a black man's
death, arguing
that the widow
had been *frail, delicate,*
while Virginia
they called *full-blooded*—
a *negress* with eyes
dark, lusterless.
They reported her
to have a black man's
appetite, a black
man's sleep,
untroubled, sound
as though from some
hard labor. She
waited for it five months,
listening to lawyers
talk about writs
and appeals
in a cell from which
she was able—
unable not—to see

clearly into the small
chamber, the scaffold
of the electric
chair, newly made
from a single tree,
the stiff leather
harnesses she would
wear. There was only
her account of it,
that they had each
taken up one
of the severed broom
handles that held
open the bedroom
windows—(salvage
of how many floors
swept, hallways,
corners), which must have
fallen to shut in
the argument, sharp
blades, one after
the other. It ended
when Virginia
shoved a towel
and with it
the woman's tongue and
some of her hair
down her throat
with a poker, she
said, to stop it.
Then she did take
a ring, a purse—some
coins, and in

the stunned
reprieve of a spring
afternoon was seen
buying penny candy,
the woman not
dead, she swore,
but quiet she had
left her as
the slow, inevitable
dissolve of those
last few hours.
The one photograph
of her—taken
at the penitentiary after
the sentence—
composes upper
body, her face, the set
of the mouth,
the inexpressible
quick in her
eyes, part unbelief,
part the look
of distance, as though
the camera's
flash crazed
the black glaze
of a sky that was to come
as it always did
with August, the strike
they would harness
for her, send
into her brain a thing
she could not have

imagined, one cloven
tongue enough
to light forever
the house she would never
again see, enough
to light the city.
She was not born
dead, but buried—
in the slow certain
strike of
conception, the quickening
into another
girlchild too black—
in a white woman's
house, her widowed
wrath and washing,
in the locket (chain
and hinge, chambered
image, perhaps
a strand of hair) she
did or did not
steal—buried
in a body having early
turned on her,
in the fullness of her own
breasts, belly,
and thighs—her grave
the bed where
she was born, the very
air, her first
drawn breath
the casting down
of a fistful of earth.

THE OCULARIST

One of the earliest
eyes was found
with the ancient
corpse of a woman
in Persia, hers
made of gold
to resemble
a small sun—
iris and sclera
chased rays—
clear testament
not to the eye,
but to the light
that had been
made go out.
The later ones
crafted of glass
I studied
and practiced
for fire-blown
beauty, learning
another fragility,
vulnerability
to the body's
heat, the way
glass shatters
inside the fleetest
fever. For
its give—
and forgiveness—
I worked then
in ivory-wax,
and after

perfecting the shape,
cloned with
paint an iris,
small blood
vessels from
filaments of red
silk, then sealed
the whole
beneath an acrylic
veneer—thin,
invisible. Mine
was always
the smaller
studio, the work
fine, lonely
as a jeweler's,
my needs
the same—a window,
a lamp, lighted
eye loupe. Half-
sculptor, half-
illustrator, I
thought for
a long time
I was crafting
something place-
saving at best,
an orbit-
warmed imposter,
elegy,
implied
narrative of loss—
flying glass

or knife,
a thumb's determined
gouge. But I
learned finally
to manipulate
the way light
played the sphere—
the pupil
seeming to dilate
from dusk or
desire—becoming
architect
not of form
but of function,
not of object
but of the seen-
self, enticing it not
to look away.
The patient's
eye took with it,
after all,
only periphery
and the perception
of depth,
asides the truest
beholding has
never required.
So I aligned
the gaze
for the whole-sighted
world, that
it might find
some small figment

of itself
contained there, already in
the brain—
I could make it
believe—the fact
of what was
not there of no
matter at all,
the final
measure of an eye's
worth, in fact,
its complete
disappearance—
and with it,
mine—into
the opposite
eye that was
such belief.

impossible bottle
(2015)

MRI

At rest, the machine makes a softer sound,
almost pleasant, something

like a lone cricket, perfected in its measure.
But the technician is too

bright, illuminant as the room—talking
with someone in the glassed

control booth about Dixie Donuts—and so
overweight I cannot

imagine she could fit herself into the tube
where she will send me

in minutes It is Friday, late afternoon;
there can't be many of us

left to see She feeds me into the mouth
of the thing, telling me

to follow the breathing directions as best I can,
and I do, for the next

three quarters of an hour, breathe in and out
and pray, curse, clench my teeth,

sorry as I have ever been for myself
and suddenly sorrier

to realize that I am the last of the many
this day; someone else's

face was just this close to the low ceiling,
someone else's worry

saw this flat whiteness. In my hand I hold
the small, bulbous call

button everyone must hold, with the same
nervous lightness, I can

imagine holding a moth—so as not to kill it
and not to let it go.

The metaphor for it metastasizes, too:
I am in the belly

of the beast, the belly of a whale, in some sterile
wilderness, desert

island, sand-blind; I am a thread in the deep
eye of a needle; in some

percussive otherworld that rises up
every time I exhale

and hold still my empty lungs. And then I come to
and settle on a tunnel,

a real one, the one they call the Paw Paw
for the nearby trees,

and a day in early June three years ago,
and I can stay in there

long enough to survive it again—artifact
of a place, a quarter mile

through a mountain in western Maryland.
You are never out

of sight of the end of it, and still you find
you do need that borrowed

flashlight you thought you could do without, its battery
feeble, jittery beam.

Mules and men died in here, hauling out
the stone to make this

passage, narrow towpath alongside a stream
of water you can hear

but cannot see. The way out is searing
and round, a worthless sun

that lights nothing but itself, and still you choose it,
the entrance behind you

just as fixed but changed, somehow, another
state, no, another country,

farther away, now, you are sure, than this.

WELL

When I first knew it, it was already a structure
of sheer sentiment,

more remnant than place, covering the old,
neglected depth it took

to get to water. My mother's uncle—whose voice
I can't recall ever

hearing—built it, the tall wall he knew to sink
there because of sycamores—

ghostly water-seekers—seemingly out
of place, and a well-eye

he must have noticed brimming with ferns. The same
water in the house

would later be made plain by comparison,
tepid, tamed by spigot

and pipe, basin and drain, our chapped hands
always in it, under it.

It is not so hard now to understand what was
for a long time unrecognizable,

a given, that source as absence of something,
a backing out of this—

pipe, house, us—all of this, so perfect
as to be invisible.

CHAIN CHAIN CHAIN

Thirty years to the day since the virgin-time:
a nephew was the ring-

bearer, the rings tied down with slick ribbons
to the small satin pillow

on which he bore them. Pretending to pray, I watched
ants crawl across his shined shoes.

The pastor who declared it is long dead from cancer.
My brother as well;

that morning he came stoned, his hair long,
aviator sunglasses

blinding mirrors; and the brother-in-law and the in-laws,
my own father, all dead.

The friend who would later put a pillow over
her face and shoot herself

through it, knew what I wanted, and sent it wrapped
in butcher paper:

a Mexican wedding dress, white on white
embroidery, stitches dense,

intricate—the seamstress's signature a single
black strand of her hair

sewed into the yoke. It was, indeed, perfect.
It is. The April air is

chill as it has ever been. I dance to *chain*
chain chain before I take it

off again and feed it to the fire I have set
for this. There was

a garden, a watchful gardener, a small
cement pool, fat carp, a statue

of a little girl carved into her dress of stone,
her face abstracted by moss.

WEATHER

for Kent

They said they had no category for it,
a hybrid thing they christened

and numbered anyway. The meteorologists
couldn't help but be

delirious; its center massive and slow,
its ocean-born body

coming inland then as bodies, one winter,
one tropical, a conjoined

thing no one had ever seen; how healthy
it was, they marveled, how

determined—part cyclone, blizzard, part hurricane,
tornado, all of it,

all of it applied. They pointed to maps,
measurements and charts;

they struggled to track it, predict what it
might do. Already numberless

outages, closures. Here—you had catalogued,
stored up what we might need—

batteries, candles, canned fruit, bottled water,
matches, the transistor

radio. We listened to the wind;
we waited. You were more

restless than I was, going out again
and again onto the porch,

to see for yourself, leaning into it,
almost as though to dare it,

test it, touch the hem of it, or let it
touch you; before you knew,

you knew it would spare us.

ORNITHOGRAPHY: PREPARING THE STUDY SKIN

People know to call him when they find one—
a heron collapsed on the bank

of the canal, a cardinal having mistaken
glass for air, the dove

I found in our garden. He keeps them all in a freezer
in the lab, bagged in plastic,

a random, patient flock—until he finds
an hour on a weekend afternoon,

a Sunday like this one the quietest, the science building
empty, lab serene

beneath the hum of florescence. The process
is the same no matter the bird,

though a starling has the toughest flesh, he says,
and a mourning dove like mine

the thinnest, like tissue paper. He lays out the implements,
simple and few, tweezers,

scalpel, scissors, some thread: First, he places cotton down
the throat to absorb the blood.

After breaking the humerus bone, he loosens the wings
from the body, makes a simple

incision, then, straight down the belly to peel back
skin from the muscles

encasing organs, turns the body inside out.
He scoops the brain, the way

he might a yolk from an egg—scoops out the eyes,
surprisingly large, given

the size of the skull. He wants me to see how it is
translucent as porcelain,

holds it up to show me how the light
passes through. The body

mass, the brain, the eyes he replaces with cotton.
The wings he secures

to the sides of the body, finishing by fixing
crossed feet and bill neatly

with sewing thread, then binding the whole to a stick
like something about to be

burned alive. It is, after all, not meant
to remind but to instruct,

he says—so that we are allowed to see what was
kept from us, the color phases

of the screech owl, the very fringe that soundproofed
deadliest flight, here, touch it—

all of it prepared, collected, labeled, and kept
for this in narrow drawers—

part catalogue, part library, part still-formed twin
of the garden where I found it.

BLOOD-GROOVE

My brother was angry; I understand that
now, the Boy Scouts my mother

led all trying to build fires inside circles
she had taught them to make

of stone. With no choice but to bring me with her,
she left me alone

to gather my own rocks and tinder; I recall
dry grass and twigs, skeletal

leaves, the small cardboard drawer with the one
wooden match I was

allowed, the rasp of the strike, my fire the first
to blaze and with such brightness

I could not help but call out from it—to my mother,
to all the boys. He drew

his knife, held it by the tip, then threw it
for all he was worth,

shaft and blade, blood-groove, and bone handle, sailing
end over end, until

it found the outer orbit of my left eye,
where I will always be

able to measure the size of its strike, the depth
of its impression

that of a grain of rice. I never asked—
and will never know

what were his chances, what was his aim, by
how much he might have

missed his mark, or how close he came.

INFUSION SUITE

1

The nurse puts on the protective gown for this one,
sky-blue, crepe paper-like. She asks again
for me to verify name, date of birth,
checking what I say against the information
on the small plastic bag she shows to me
before hanging it upside down, its contents
impossibly clear, benign looking
as water coursing the clearest bore—
umbilical-like, that almost invisible line.
The trees outside the tall window appear
still full with summer, crows' flight—more
like drunken tumbling—something to see
while I agree that *yes, yes, this is me.*

2

The poplars outside this place an old stand,
their trunks rise, slender nudes that sway in a rush
of wind and sun. At the trees' edge, someone
has hung feeders to distract us from ourselves,
and so I don't look at her when she says
to the screen of her computer that my blood
numbers are good, better, in fact, than last

time. Hour after hour, we watch birds circle
the plastic cylinders of sunflower seed,
cling to the caged cakes of suet swinging
from tall hooked poles—not unlike ours, I like
to think, their source of flight gravity-measured,
a given, too—and we are all radiant with it.

3

The surgery was a flash
fire in the yard, folks

nearly delirious
with rakes and hoses, their

faces hot with it.
This place is the slow

burn they watch, if they do,
at a safer distance, as

they might a neighbor's field
smoldering, glad it's

not their own, their concern
now the direction of

the wind, a chance of rain.

4

Leonard, he shrugs the name patch on his shirt;
his cancer back after a good year and a half;
it's worse this time; then tells me just as much

a matter of fact he is a mechanic
at the collision place, his specialty the under

-carriage of a car after a wreck,
realignment, the stuff nobody ever sees
and will never notice unless—no, until—

it gets out of whack; he's lucky, though,
his brother's bone marrow a match, the one
he had not spoken to in thirty years;

he will go into work tomorrow, has to, that new guy—
he shrugs again—some brand new kind of stupid.

5

I am not this, not here, this time. I am
what I mistook for a shadow

in our walled garden, gathered beneath the concrete
bench, concrete also the sky,

like the cold, sorrowful bottom of something; it is
a collared shadow, though—a stray cat

I see us feeding in the afternoon. And I
will watch it eat from a dish

on the back stoop, then bathe in the open doorway
of the garage, in that narrow shaft

of afternoon light, where I will be also,
and also behind it, where I am

the body of light that swings from the rafters.

6

The trees redden beneath it, before loss,
becoming livid with this: rain, cold, windless,
shadowless the light, the sky a low

opalescence. This one a quieter day,
the room empties earlier. I eat
a bowl of soup from the table I make

of my lap. Later, I will win at scrabble,
studying my sorry trough of letters—
CAUSE double its worth, though, and I puzzle it

with UZ—as in Job, as in the land of—triple—
cheating, really, but we agree we will
let it go this time, all my words small

but costly, and my accounting of them perfect.

7

gray on gray this

scale the woman's

face her counts so

low her lips blanched

to this parchment

where I write her

even her eyes

faded paling

to a sameness moth-like

her expression

the sameness shifting

fog that pretends

to know no noon

8

I know the nurses' names by now, recognize
several patients, our familiarity
with each other that of folks on the same bus,
its slowness a shared slow-jolt alarm, the lumbering

maddening, then numbing. A woman I have never
seen, purple-turbaned, prefers jaundiced leaves,
birdless feeders someone forgot to fill
to any of us. I have chosen to look out

that window at what passes for the world.
We all have. What we do not know about
each other can go unspoken; our old ordinary

means nothing here, and we know already
the ordinary that this is—and is—.

9

The old woman next to me does not speak
all day, not even to the young girl who came

to be with her, a granddaughter, perhaps,
with nails painted the same electric blue

she used to paint her grandmother's nails,
and perhaps she was the one who plaited

the single tight gray braid—a pinned, frayed

aura around her head. Her eyes occluded,
clouded over, the older woman appears

to look me in the eye, though, to hold me in
an iron-steady gaze, the cataracts

small blinds she has early drawn down,
defiant, and she stands behind having done it.

10

The Mayan calendar ran out
a week ago, and still

this year ends on what we insist
is an eve, the day

ledge-like, gate-like, a transom.
A man in the waiting

room opens a penknife and begins
to scrape away at what

I have mistaken for his palm—
a lottery ticket,

scratch-and-win, and he is
delirious with it, this

small chance (why not?) all.

11

We have come in from what was earlier
predicted to be ice, the steady pour instead
washing away last scraps of snow. The man
across the way opens his lunch: a block of cheese,
saltines, a jar of sweet pickles. He chooses
from among them thoughtfully; the excess syrup
he lets drip back into the jar before removing
his choice from the blade of his penknife. All this

tires him. When he is finished, he covers his eyes
with his jacket's empty sleeve. I see it is too easy
a metaphor, and though nothing will wake him
all afternoon, I will not mistake his
loosely sleeved sleep for anything else.

12

I bring a tray of puddings
to share on my

last day. Each cup is different,
some topped with berries,

some with peppermints.
I give everyone

a small wooden spoon,
the kind I recall

from elementary school
birthday parties,

something you use once,
throw away,

think nothing of.

MORTUARY MAKE-UP ARTIST

The medicine cabinet has become her, her face
a small door she opens

and closes—its store her closeted cures,
prescriptions for sorrow,

a vial for the self in beauty school, the corpses
she trains for—her body

the wall, wall socket, and drain. Everyday
she wears a smock, wide,

gaping pockets, carries a rigid, plastic
caddy—a neatened arsenal

of tiny scissors, tweezers, a razor, lotions,
and liners for their eyes,

their lips. The penny on the tongue is her idea,
she thinks, a coppery

lozenge not unlike the sadness she savors
to spend and spend like this—

this one, insoluble syllable.

A THOUGHT

Somewhere in her brain there is a cognitive
map, a constellation

of place-cells sunk deep in gray matter—and there,
a man, the one she told

no to, refuses to disappear with that
long-ago summer where

she borrowed a house, as though to borrow him,
or time. There, she has

planned it, the farewell pleasant she knows he will
argue against. He likes

even the word *mistress*, the hiss of it,
its gloss a lingering kiss.

She draws a deep tub, lights candles along
the edge, water releasing

steam like guilt, grief, relief. He is behind her
in the bath, saying something,

nothing, his hands warm and wet encircling
not her shoulders now

but her throat with what the brain might not have
stored at all—so close

to ordinary the gesture. He lets them
linger like the thought

he has or does not have, about what he
could but would not do,

one finger tracing the hollow notch that knits
her collarbones together,

for the last time, tracing it. He will sleep well
and rise before her

in the morning. He has brought fresh cherries
in a paper bag; it rustles

with the movement of his hand as he replaces
each one with its pit,

methodical such capable hunger.
He will return to his wife,

his children, the shop where he sells suet
and seed, to the bell

he hung so that it tinkles sweetly when
someone enters, enticed

by the brightly painted houses for bats
and birds. *Come in, Come in,*

it says to them, and again, now, to her,
as he smiles from behind

the counter, just a thought, enjoying how
it does not fail to become him.

CYST

She had once had an abortion, she said, and later
an affair with a married man,

then another, her solitude always
uneasy, her body

lonely for something nameless as they had been,
or as she made them.

She said it began as pressure not quite pain,
and they found it outside

the womb, clinging to an ovary, having
conceived of itself.

When they removed it, they told her she could see it
if she wanted to:

just a curiosity with teeth, hair, and nails. Odd
but benign, the doctor

said, most always benign, nodding toward it
as though it could agree

with him, as though that were the fact,
the whole of it: curious

mistake a body can make.

FAST

Her daughters were born fast, three in a row,
the older two the ordinary

disappointment most girls are to their fathers,
the third one *God's child,*

she said, declaring it so; *bird-stupid,* he called it,
slow as a log chain

through mud. The house she would never leave
was on the steepest street

in town, and the older girls learned there to be fast
on skates and sleds, and then

they were old enough for the married men, so easy
and fast and grateful—

no cleaning, no fights—just cars and the steep
slant of a summer night,

and the quick lie that an hour can be, the slickest one
after babysitting

his children, the road where they parked the one
with all the switchbacks—

deer dead in the ditches—and they took to it
like breaking into a house

just for the fun of it, like stealing someone
else's air, someone else's

darkness, the stuff even the smartest woman
will not miss. They were

her only wildness, and she would lie awake
for the hint of its return,

some man's smoke fast in its hair—
God's child dead asleep.

IMPOSSIBLE BOTTLE

◆

I recall it as a lens—thick, dimensioned—
its neck the stoppered

threshold to a chamber, the chamber
an encapsulation

of the ship, a clipper, graceful and lean, its sails
pristine, the delicate

threads of its rigging. That kind of green glass
my mother had seen

only on weather vanes or as decorative part
of a lightning rod, the glass's

survival sculpted proof of a strike that
had not yet happened.

◆

When I was small, we drove only one time
to the ocean, all of us

afraid of that kind of water, that horizon.
The day we left for home,

she told me to fill a bottle with air, to steal
some away as a souvenir

to open and breathe one winter night
when my attic bedroom

window would seal me in and threaten to let me
forget that day, its perilous air.

◆

And she recalls exactly how the ship
got in there—suspended,

bottled against wind and water, driftless
in the dead sea of the cupboard

where she'd keep it; she was young then
and had never seen the ocean.

She was already wearing a ring on a chain
around her neck to hide it

from her mother. The ghost ship's arrival
was at the hands of a man

at the fair who took her money to let her
watch him slip the slim,

collapsed body into the bottle and then—
with a single practiced tug

of thread—raise it to the hereafter
of her house that is sealed

now as she says it must be for the very old.
She rarely opens a window,

even on the mildest day—impossible
as it has ever been

to worry too much about the wind.

THE SCAR

The fainting she cannot recall—or the strike
of her face against

the table's edge—only the waking, the blood
in her eye from the brow-

bone, her mother's face so close to hers
she could not see her.

The remedy: to fill the gash with soot
from the stove—a quick

staunching, the firebox still hot with live coals.
The bleeding would stop,

and the wound heal over to this—palest
blue, reminiscent

of an eyelash tattooed, prettied as though meant,
something she might have

chosen for herself. She does not have to
tell it for me to see

a morning's shimmering heat, the rooms of that child's
house—her mother seeing her

the way she sees me through this indelible
sill of ash—

and behind it the fire that had given the stove-eye
its brightest-ever aura.

secure the shadow
(2012)

IT

My cousin liked to dangle me upside down
 by the ankles, my aunt's crossed in thick disapproval

at eye level, the world gone wrong, blood fallen
 in a dizzy rush to my ears until, almost

made afraid, I heard his familiar laughter
 as though from some sealed depth beneath me.

Until he is called up,
 Vietnam is sound

broadcast: the voice of evening
 news a televised census

of the dead, the rising number
 bodiless, somehow, nameless

narcosis of fact. Or it
 is still, in black and white:

water buffalo, the sullen
 work of drowned fields;

a monk sitting cross-legged
 in placid meditation

of the self as fire, eyes
 and mouth closed-calm part of it.

The doll arrived at Christmastime, halfway
 through my cousin's first tour of duty,

addressed to me, the narrow cardboard box
 decorated with delicate chrysanthemums,

her face visible beneath a pale caul
        of tissue paper. I lifted her out,

delighted with her strangeness, her red dress
        of real silk slit at the sides to the hip,

her conical grass hat. But I could imagine
        no part for her in the plots of my other dolls,

no dream house or car, no man. She was sewn
        tight into her only dress, her form,

a full grown woman's, rigid inside it, posture
        strict, unbending, her gaze untranslatable.

She had traveled across the ocean in the belly
        of a plane, in dark storage with letters, packages,

those flagged caskets. She was not dead, I decided,
        but made blind, and with no way to tell it,

no tongue in her mouth, her body hollow, soundless.

And then it is children
        running toward me, the faint,

rain-shimmering shadows before them
        stunted, those of early

afternoon, and a girl, naked,
        the scorched disfigurement

of her back unseen, inescapable
        as what had been the road

behind her, its vanishing point
    consumed inside an earthbound

cloud, her scream—seared
    aperture to something

the image cannot document.

The small box of ashes neatly buried,
    my cousin would drive me home

from my father's funeral, that mile
    the only conversation I would be able

to recall between the two of us alone,
    his summer visits for years brief and shallow—

the distance easy to blame. He would be
    matter of fact, telling me about

the Agent Orange he'd breathed, believed revenant
    in a tumor, the cancer in his throat—

its remission. Not a day had passed
    when he hadn't smelled it, tasted it—

the *it* slender and exact as a compass needle—
    he would say as though to the road ahead,

or suddenly blind to it, his eyes, tongue, throat,
    his voice I would hear burning with

a knowing beyond memory—wordless,
    imageless—the body's own account.

ANIMAL FUNERALS, 1964

That summer, we did not simply walk through
    the valley of the shadow of death;

we set up camp there, orchestrating funerals
    for the anonymous, found dead: a drowned mole—

its small, naked palms still pink—a crushed
    box turtle, black snake, even a lowly toad.

The last and most elaborate of the burials—
    a common jay, identifiable

but light, dry, its eyes vacant orbits.
    We built a delicate lychgate of willow fronds,

supple and green, laced through with chains of clover.
    Roles were cast: preacher, undertaker—

the rest of us a straggling congregation
    reciting what we could of the psalm

about green pastures as we lowered the shoebox
    and its wilted pall of dandelions

into the shallow grave one of us had dug
    with a serving spoon. That afternoon,

just before September and school, when we would
    again become children, and blind to all

but the blackboard's chalky lessons, the back
    of someone's head, and what was, for a while

longer, the rarer, human death—there, in the heat-shimmered
    trees, in the matted grasses where we stood,

even in the slant of humid shade, we heard wingbeat,
    slither, buzz, and birdsong, a green racket rising

to fall as though in a sublime dirge that was real,
    and not part of our many necessary rehearsals.

FIRST DEATH

Now, the first of my father's maiden aunts
        was dying, the frail kindest of the three,

her bed set up downstairs in the formal parlor
        where the coffin soon would follow, the room

darkened, curtains drawn against the day
        for no good reason I could see, an afternoon's

wasting outside equally terrible,
        all inside now defined by the other

aunts' hushed fussing, the smell of her breathing,
        of cloves, pain, of something unidentifiable

just beneath her nightgown, the soft veneer
        of talcum's dissolve. My mother asked me

to crush ice, something useful, she said,
        but I saw in it a way out as I wrestled cubes

from aluminum trays, wrapped them in a dishcloth
        to crush on the concrete stoop out back.

Alone then with the fattening shadows of sheets
        on the line, the sickbed filled with wind, I fell

to my task, sudden unfamiliar delight
        in the heft of the hammer, in a sound

as of bones breaking, the sense perhaps of some part
        giving way, a finger, maybe, a tooth,

fragile hand, delicate foot. I opened
        the cloth to dainty slivers I swaddled again

for her forehead, saving some, as I had been
    instructed, in a china cup, for her to hold

in her mouth. My mother took it from me,
    and from the threshold, I could see

my great-aunt's face abstracted in half-light,
    her mouth a deeper shadow closing—

what she might have understood
    of my labor already vanished on her tongue.

ZENITH

Younger sister he suffers, I have just turned three,
          eating supper with my brother: in the photograph

he wears cowboy boots, dungarees, pajama top—
          his head shaved close to bald, six-shooter holstered

at the small table we share every night.
          I am also in boots, hand-me-down rifle

at the ready by my plate. My helmet
          from another war, its netting I'll weave

with leaves, broomsedge, pine fronds, anything
          to camouflage me, confuse the enemy

the way he has taught me, whispering *listen,*
          there, listen—Japanese, Germans, Apaches,

Yankees unseen, everywhere. We don't know
          how little we have to fear in our small

country town, for years its one traffic light
          a mere yellow pulse benign as a firefly's.

The enemies of this place—drought, hail, an early
          or late frost—refuse our aim, the smallest

human industry defined by the health
          of tobacco fluming in the fields that surround us.

I can't tell what's on our plates, but if it's Monday,
          meatloaf and mashed potatoes, Tuesday,

pork chops, fried apples. But our attentions
          are not on the meal, not on the camera, or

our mother, but on something just beyond
the picture's border captioned with the date,

January 1960: the black-and-white
Zenith, tuned to Davy Crockett or the Rifleman—

easy heroes. We can't know what we're armed
against or training for—another war

for Cronkite to narrate, cataloging
the dead nightly in a country we've not yet heard of,

or suspicious rustlings, wind in the thicket
of his body, my brother's illness

and too-early death still years away—
with unnumbered other captures between,

like this one: small, humorous,
the flash from my mother's camera

caught bouncing off the wall and door behind us,
still-sudden backlight to all we cannot see.

OLD ELEMENTARY

Terrified or furious, he would call me:
        it's in there, he'd swear, *in the old elementary—*

desperate to blame something—asbestos,
        radiation, unhappiness itself—

to place, displace the cancer onto the first school
        he despised, in the despised small town

where we grew up. I drive past it every time
        I go back, the building abandoned

years ago by all but vagrant pigeons.
        The utter childlessness of the playground

fronts it, lifeless swings, foot-worn furrows
        beneath, once slick from use, almost closed over,

a cicatrix of dandelions and wire grass.
        Then the stern-faced architecture, strict dormers,

the heavy, recessed doors through which we entered,
        two stories, walls all windows, every one

he stared out from, away from hissing radiators,
        oil-polished wood floors, crayon wax,

pencil shavings, the chronic dust of lead,
        chalk, faint fear—and the long hallways

not hard for me to imagine empty,
        dimly lit, where I recall waiting for him

one cavernous afternoon, when all
        the other children had been released, and he

was kept after, inside, *in there,* for punishment,
        in there for some small forgotten thing.

CALF KILLINGS

The first time, they were clearly slaughtered,
        dissembled in the mauling, bodies strewn
mangled over the pasture as though whatever
        attacked them had fallen into a fury
at what it did not find in them. The men
        speculated—*wolves*, they said, but there were no
wolves anymore, or *panthers*, all killed off
        long ago in the stories of dead men,

so they debated but agreed on bear—
        set traps that yawned, gleaming and clean, empty
for weeks. And so another season came
        and went before another field nearby
turned up littered with dead, though this time
        the bodies were unmarked, almost as though
they had simply lain down in their shadows
        before rain. But it must have been the calves

who had churned the frozen ground alongside
        the fenceline, worse in the corners, evidence
of a shared and violent end. The veterinarian
        could say for certain only that they had suffered
pneumonia, brought on by nights spent
        in icy rain, and while no one quite
believed it as cause, they turned to what
        was left to do, gathering the remains

to burn. The only survivor of that last night
        was a mule, moon blind and grazing calmly, ignored
old among them. But when the fire had become
        one thick, impenetrable column, the men watched
as it drifted late toward them—pulling behind it
        the rippling wake of a ragged shadow like a tedious
ghost—as though again reluctant witness,
        even to this necessary warmth.

DOCUMENTARY

After the bullet had halted in the brain
        and with it the breathing, my cousin recalls
his father slitting the hog's throat right there
        in the lot to begin the cleansing bleed.
This had happened for so many falls,
        he said the soil before the trough had been

changed by it, and while still the stuff of mud
        and sand, of hoofprints frozen into deep-cloven
molds, its color, its texture, had assumed
        a chocolaty depth, obvious, ignored
once the freshness of the smell receded into cold—
        seepage settling like a thicker rain.

◆

The documentary opens
        with the photograph they thought

would capture the kill—the wild boar's
        thousand-pound body strung up,

hoghook attached to the backhoe the men
        had brought into the swamp in order

to prove, measure, then bury
        this thing long-rumored, glimpsed,

heard, its size given scale
        by the man—posed smiling

as for any photograph—
        made small beside it.

◆

The whole of them thriving after all,
    they appeared agreeable somehow to it—
the calm way a hog turned out roamed close
    all summer, the bell piercing its ear
unnecessary. (He reminds me that theirs
    is a hunger easily satisfied, the browsing

turning up anything that grew or landed close:
    insects, eggs, lizards, snakes, young birds,
and moles—everything rooted, bulbs and tubers,
    and with them the congregation of decay,
worms and beetles, a lung-shot doe some hunter
    gave up following discovered with equal delight.)

It entered the lot without real protest,
    showing joy in the slop and corn, the confines
of the trough. Perhaps an understanding came
    in the suckling, that the afterworld of their bodies
was fused with the ones turned feral, escaped to the hidden
    sounders and the wild odor of the hive.

◆

The narrative, already virile,
    the town nearby embellished—

how he heard before he saw it,
    killed it with a single shot

or surely it would have killed him—
    how the creature had all the features

of a wild boar in its sheer size,
the coat mud-rimed wire, tusks thick

as a man's forearm, but also how
it bore sure signs that someone had once

owned it, claimed it in the docked tail,
in the ear's notch—deep, deliberate.

◆

My mother says the day was decided
after a week's worth of heavy frost,
persimmons stricken sweet, the dawn
shadowless. The axe angled gnomon-like
but hourless from the block. Smoke
from the scalding fire so finely laced
the air it was as inextricable
from it as the sound of a blade

sharpening, its measure breathlike, the fragrance
of a whetted edge mingling iron
with the smoke. The world outside the pen
was slatted again, redefined in thick slices
of dawn, and with its slow reemergence
of color, the tattered remnants of the garden

returned. The sage patch still dense by the woodshed
volunteered thicker and healthier
every year—and the house from which the children
spilled with slop and corn, their screams coming sharp,
voices rising, pale wisps feathering
from the heat of small, determined mouths.

◆

The town celebrated, paraded,
the children wearing plastic snouts

and little ears, holding paper cones
of cotton candy, greasy sacks

of popcorn. Following the marching band,
someone's tractor pulled a float

that carried a living tableau
of the scene they had been told

they could stop imagining:
a blood-covered man overcome

by the long-feared boar—in paper mâché
a quick, rough rendering.

◆

All of it was worth the work she says:
nothing wasted—hocks, hams, chops, fatback,
bacon, even the ears, feet, intestine,
tongue, the heart, even the brain that would be
in the morning scrambled to the plural *brains-*
and-eggs, salted, peppered; her mother
shushing the children not to think about it.
The learned ritual of that day would define

winter—the body going from fall's quick,
purgatorial fattening to an anatomy
segmented, ordered first in the meatbox, hams
and shoulders packed tight in salt, kept in the hold

of the smokehouse, where later they would be hung, crowded there;
        she says its eaves steamed night after night
against the early winter sky—a small house
        that would not succumb to the fire it had inside it.

◆

But doubt would suspend the story,
        possibility upon

whispered possibility,
        then a small certain voice,

then two: they could have mistaken it
        for the one still in the swamp,

something they had never known.
        Only three men saw the body

after all, and them not from
        around here, the photograph

a made thing—no proof
        in such small witness.

◆

So much revision in the rendering, in the precise
        economy of a slow, graveless decay,
some of what remained of the body distilled,
        disappeared in the snaps and potatoes—seasoned
the greens, the soup, assumed the form of lard
        in the bucket, of soap by the sink. Relics of the body

once carried, obeyed, the feet, cloven and delicate,
        my mother learned to pickle alongside
cucumbers, beets, and peaches; no longer gravity
        bound, they floated weightless, suspended in the gallon
glass jar like curiosities in a medical museum—
        or specimens preserved for study.

◆

And so the documentary
        closes with the men's

return, scientists
        among them this time.

They wear rubber gloves,
        boots to the hip, black

masks. No resurrection, this—
        inquiry an insult

to the swamp's slow recollection
        of what has already

disappeared among them,
        the fact of that.

◆

It drifts through the dead finish of the thicket—
        swamp and understory—shared threshold
with predictable clearings, lots, coops,
        cellars, lofts, and cages, a house, the shadows
neat, obedient. One form reforms,
        resolves, survival more than the memory

of muscle and space, more than the summoning
    back of time, the body and brain indivisible,
changing around what has changed and will
    again, penumbral noon and after
noon, the way the wind rises as something
    recalled, called, and recalled.

THE PRESENT TENSE

There will be a worse day. He will live long
    enough not to know me at all, and the turn

toward it, begun this hour with recognition,
    has slowed to a measureless stare, worse

than the wordless pauses common now;
    he concentrates on me, direct and quiet,

the way light concentrates, falling through
    a window to the floor. I hold his gaze

until I am considering the surface
    of his eyes the way I might the dulling

surface of a pond drought-shrunken, clouded
    over with dust and pollen. But there is light

enough to see my face mirrored
    weakly, small, infant in the pupils

as though from some great distance. Finally, I ask him
    what he is thinking about—or if he is

remembering something he'd like to tell me,
    and at last he nods saying yes, he is; he is

remembering his daughter, naming me
    in the third person as though I am not

the one asking, as though I am the one—not dying,
    but already mourned, and he has survived me

long enough to find solace in a memory.
    And I, as I have always known myself,

am fallen away then from the present
    tense into reminiscence—the lucid *was*.

CAUSE

We dress him for the fire in what he might have
    chosen for himself. Arranging neckties

on the bed, bright-shimmering as a peacock's
    display, we match, consider, consult—busying

ourselves. The forms we have already filled out
    in duplicate, triplicate, the death certificate

ordered—rote questions, designated
    lines for time and cause, time itself

not among the choices, the *failure*
    to thrive standard they explain, a diagnosis

I've heard before but only for the newborn
    that refuse without cause to suckle.

We have found his birth certificate
    in the labyrinth of a desk that had been

his father's before him, tight pigeonholes
    and boxes within drawers, the bottom one

as deep as a baby's crib, laden
    with banknotes, ledgers, vaccination records,

deeds, loans, pocket knives, dogtags, tax returns,
    eyeglasses, a fist-thick bunch of keys—

vanished doors—all of it a catalog
    of balances, the satisfied, useless,

broken, sentimental, saved for no real
    purpose but this, the cluttered consolation

of ended causes, the hours that do not burn.

JUBILATION

for Betty Adcock

The rear wall of her house all glass, the garden
defined the living room with its small stand

of paper birches, a narrow stream, the hillside
that confined it—all quick with flight and shadows

of flight—cardinals, thrushes, juncos, doves,
sometimes a heron, a hawk. She said

the birds must believe, if belief applied in such,
that the mirrored trees were ahead when they flew

into the reflection that was her house,
unaware that what killed or stunned was more

than glass—the misdirected flight we all
take sometimes into the place just left behind.

And when she found a bird tangled in ivy,
she put it in a shoebox in a closet;

there sometimes it would return to itself—
the enclosed hour she had come to imagine

it perceived only as a healing fugue
of darkness, another night that had indeed

passed not so much unlike all the others.
The lid removed then not to death

but to sudden afternoon and the briefest
moment of stillness before the rush

of lifting up and out, a quickening
reabsorbed at once into the oblivion

of a world having gone on bright and raucous
    without it, no worse for the absence, perhaps—

but surely that was jubilation she heard
    in the cicadas' immediate flourish

of sound, as though the hour itself had been
    restored with the bird it had moved through.

FOR ONCE

I had many times walked past it: crowded
    stand of mixed woods where a field used to be,

self-ordained survivors of a place
    having gone unnoticed long enough

for them to volunteer: maples, scrub pines,
    some cedars—a blood beech leaved even

in winter, little remarkable either
    for ruin or beauty. And then something, in there,

caused me to pause, sounds a wakeful house
    can make—the restlessness of a slumberous

body shifting in bed, the strike of a match,
    foot doubtful on a stair, kindling catching,

water from a spigot, fatwood hiss.
    Or all of it the acoustics of emptiness—

needles of ice ticking on abandoned glass,
    a porch swing's chained keening. But it was habit

to find the familiar in that shifting architecture,
    its trueness not finally in the measure

and level of some human past, or possible,
    but in that present quickening—wind-cast

shadows of sound and soundlessness, unseen,
    unknowable, and, for once, enough.

LIFEGUARD

She perches high on the stand, gleaming whistle
        dangling, on her suit a dutiful,

faded red cross. Mine her only life
        to guard, she does for a while watch

the middle-aged woman who has nothing better
        to do than swim laps in the Y's indoor pool

on a late Friday afternoon. I am slow,
        though, boring, length after predictable

length of breaststroke or the duller lap
        of elementary backstroke perfectly

executed within the taut confines
        of the brightly buoyed lane. So she abandons me

to study split-ends, hangnail, wristwatch,
        until—the body of the whistle cupped

loosely in her palm—her head nods toward
        shallow dreams. I've never felt so safe in my life,

making flawless, practiced turns, pushing, invisible,
        to reenter my own wake, reverse it.

FLOCKING THEORY

At dusk each winter evening, in the half hour
	before they must relinquish sky to night,

starlings quicken, flock in forms—symmetries
	shifting—the likenesses so fast and fluid

I can't hold on to any one before
	it dissolves into another, and I

have taught myself to accept the seamless
	recreations not as uneasy

whimsy but as the musings of a lucid soul
	or the disclosures of God: the wind

itself made seen, the shade a shadow casts.
	No one knows for certain what controls this,

the flock moving by space measured and kept—
	strict distances—between the bodies.

But the birds, I like to think, are having
	none of theory, anyway, whatever

it may be, none of me, abandoning
	themselves instead to the invariable

bliss of what is, the fact of flying
	manifest in every changing figure:

one enormous wing, a waterfall
	of bees, a murmurous curtain falling

to rise as smoke, a funnel cloud,
	helix, an arm, its empty sleeve.

figure studies
(2008)

THE MANNEQUIN ABOVE *MAIN STREET MOTORS*

When the only ladies' dress shop closed,
she was left on the street for trash, unsalvageable,

one arm missing, lost at the shoulder, one leg
at the hip. But she was wearing a blue-sequined negligee

and blonde wig, so they helped themselves to her
on a lark—drunken impulse—and for years kept her

leaning in a corner, beside an attic
window, rendered invisible. The dusk

was also perpetual in the garage below,
punctuated only by bare bulbs hung close

over the engines. An oily grime coated
the walls, and a decade of calendars promoted

stock-car drivers, women in dated swimsuits,
even their bodies out of fashion. Radio distorted

there; cigarette smoke moaned, the pedal steel
conceding to that place a greater, echoing

sorrow. So, lame, forgotten prank, she remained,
back turned forever to the dark storage

behind her, gaze leveled just above
anyone's who could have looked up

to mistake in the cast of her face fresh longing—
her expression still reluctant figure for it.

LATIN TEACHER

Seamed stockings, sensible shoes, cardigan
buttoned all the way to the top, she greets

each of them by name as they enter her classroom
rebellious, identical. They want Italian,

French, a younger teacher—anything
but this woman fluent in a language

that will not travel—the deep south of her vowels
slow as the minute hand on the grinding clock

behind her. Her hair is braided and coiled, contained
in a bun substantial as a hornets' nest—ashen gray.

But their mothers also were made to take it—
translations all the more hated for being inherited.

Then they are assigned to her table in the din
of the dining room, where she directs them

to eat even popsicles with a knife and fork.
She serves fried chicken by inquiring if they prefer

to *walk* or *fly*. And they learn to choose the leaner wing
because they believe it pleases her. At Halloween,

in the darkened gymnasium, beside the tub of water
where girls bob for apples, she sits in a small

booth to tell fortunes, peers into their palms:
esto perpetua, whispering again

and again the same lie of a life so long
they don't listen—their attentions lost

instead in the swung shock of her hair
let down into luminescence, brushing the floor

like a curtain just closing behind her.

WARMBLOODS

Tails, manes, and forelocks painstakingly braided,
they have submitted all afternoon to the saddle—

the bit's dull, metallic taste. Now, outside
the close, dark stalls—hay fragrant in the loft above—

they hold still for hard, sharp blasts of water,
bodies steaming, shuddering beneath last,

dutiful brushes. Thousand-pound creatures,
generations broken, their only wildness is this

ninety pounds of girl—hard hat of velvet
veneer, heels neatly down, the controlled, meant

growl behind the ear before the jump. Tonight
while the girls sleep, they will be allowed the fog-white

pasture, where the deer, unafraid of sharing
this fate, seek the careful grass and easier salt—

and the warmbloods will roll on their backs, the joy
of the earth behind them, hooves loosed, pounding soundless sky.

LIVING NATIVITY

They have filled roles from Willie Loman to Lear,
from Atticus Finch to the Gentleman Caller,

convincing themselves and each other that they are
to be believed. So now as the innkeeper,

Joseph, the kings, and shepherds—charcoal-bearded—
they have rehearsed their easy entrances,

when and how to kneel, where to place the myrrh
and frankincense. But the virgin is always

a secret until the last hour, her identity known
only by the headmaster, who has chosen her,

and the housemother, who whisks away the prettiest
from the candlelit Christmas banquet

to brush her already-brushed hair and drape her
in della robbia blue—made soft by years

of other girls. She is placed as they were
center stage where a spotlight reveals her

gazing marblelike into the manger—nothing
for her to know beyond the fact of being

chosen, nothing for her to practice,
having learned already this stillness.

ORGANIST

They know he doesn't want them—and love him for it.
His hair uncut, uncombed, all his clothes worn soft,

he is thoughtless about the body he inhabits,
and they are part of his denial of it.

They line up around the chapel for the year's
audition, desperate to be chosen for the choir,

where they learn the proper way to open their mouths
and breathe, wear the crimson-collared robes,

and ascend the dim spiral of stairs into the loft.
He entices a few to study the guitar or flute—

slim, bright, divisible—says the organ
is a jealous thing, selfish as God to demand

he come to it in this ornate house where he is
always cold and the leaded glass casts

dim, rose-gold translations of light. Yet, long after
the last bell, they will listen to his sustaining practice,

sleep-confusing music, uncontainable as desire.

UPPER ARCADE

In the brief hour that spans study hall and bed,
the girls—already nightgowned, barefoot—are allowed

to move between buildings on the high, narrow walkway
that couples the dormitories at the second story.

Supported from beneath by a sequence
of vaulted arches, the arcade frees them

to open air, and sometimes they lean out as though over
the railing of a ship, wind shushing the waxy clatter

of the magnolias. Or, though warned not to, they run
back and forth, lightly defiant, leaping up and up

to land quietly, spines arched as they have been taught
in dance class, the hand-polished barre and long

mirrored wall where they watched themselves learn this
now forgotten, locked in the reflection of darkness beneath them.

ORCHID ANATOMY

This evening's study the anatomy of the orchid,
the greenhouse glows—jut of glass at the third story

of the science building—a small, tended jungle
thriving in its humid room. Wearing identical

lab aprons, they lean over the misting table
or peer into the daintier air-orchids

in order to name and sketch the parts,
committing to memory the sepals, inner whorl

of petals, the column where male and female
fuse, and the sticky, stigmatic surface

of the pouting lip where birds, moths,
and bees would land if allowed this sterile

world. Each wall, even the vaulted roof
a canvas, all their breathing dissolves

into the ordered atmosphere of this
one sustained season—until, if seen

from the outside, the glass's weeping would
render them recognizable but changed,

their bodies, braids, aprons, the green leaves running
into a pleasing, impressionistic bleed.

SYNCHRONIZED SWIMMING

Prim noseclips firmly in place, hair molded,
bunned at the nape, even muscle groups schooled

into exact definitions, one body appears
cloned. Linked arm to shoulder, a female strand,

the team enters the pool supple as an otter
flowing from a river-smooth rock to gather

itself into the first of the ornamental
formations. For this, they have land-drilled—

practicing poolside when and how to move,
breathe, even their smiles choreographed.

Upside-down now to assume the vertical figure,
stillness is as much part of this execution

as motion. Hands fluttering, the scull supports
legs scissoring the air before they close,

plunging into the shimmering screen of water.
The girls' disappearance so quick, precise,

the surface tension barely perceives the clean
incisions—before they reappear with ease:

bright fragments inside a kaleidoscope
dialing inflorescent patterns of glass.

HISTORY LESSON

They have been half-listening to a lecture
on the Great Depression when the teacher

looks up, begins to talk about the president
and trout fishing—a digression, he admits,

that will not be on the test. Hoover would
catch too many trout to eat and so had

a small cement pool constructed; he'd keep
the fish for days while he calmly read at the edge

of the water, absentmindedly hand-feeding
them beefhearts brought in from Washington

as though to tame them. Later, the girls
can think of nothing else, circling the goldfish

pond, throwing bits of a dinner roll onto the surface,
the fish rising to them through water so still

their slow refusal to school is its only motion.

ESTO ABSOLUTA

Despite the hallway lined with a hundred years
of girls framed in graduation white,

they can allow themselves to imagine the detritus
of classrooms, laboratories—beakers and vials—

mingling with leaf dust, and wasps passing
unhurried through the windows' paneless grid

to nest in the halls' mute bells. Rain comes in,
snow, then slower ivy in dusky air. Pigeons,

ubiquitous, whose placid voices have long
accompanied such dreaming, enter their rooms

as though enrolled, resigned to the girls' fate,
to the blackboard's chalky refusals—latent equations,

declensions, proofs—all their failed erasures.

FUNNY VALENTINE

She had been a late and only child to parents
already old and set; none of us had ever

wanted to go inside that hushed house
and play with her, her room too neat, doll-crowded.

We did encourage her later, though, to enter
the high school talent contest—after we'd heard

her singing *My Funny Valentine* in a stall
in the girls' bathroom, reckoning the boys

would laugh, perhaps find us even prettier
in comparison. Still, we would not have predicted

those wisteria-scaled walls, the one room
we could see from the street with its windows

open year round so that greening vines entered
and birds flew in and out—*bad luck,* we thought,

bad luck. By then we were members of the ladies'
garden club, the condition of her house

and what had been its garden a monthly
refreshment of disappointment, the most

delectable complaint her parents' last
Coupe de Ville sinking in tangled orchard grass

and filled to the roof—plush front seat and rear—
with paperbacks, fat, redundant romances

she had not quite thrown away—*laughable,*
we laughed, *unphotographable*—with wild restraint.

OLD PROOF

Sometimes we saw her on the junk-burdened
porch, her body long indistinguishable

from its house. If she acknowledged us,
it was with a wave that said go on, *go on,*

she was fine. The man who serviced the furnace
told us she'd saved at least thirty years' worth

of catalogs, phone books, newspapers—walls
lost behind thick stacks rising to the ceilings—

that the smell was of damp paper and ink and that throughout
the soundless house, all she'd left herself were the strictest

of paths, like a worm's slow maze through those words
she kept, old proof of us, our crowded world.

PIANO FIRE

How she must have dreaded us and our sweaty coins,
more than we hated practice, the lessons,

scales, the winter-hot parlor, arthritic
hands, the metronome's tick. She lectured

to us about the history of the piano:
baby and concert grand, spinet and player

had come across oceans in the holds of ships,
across continents in mule-drawn wagons,

heavier than all the dead left behind. On her face
we could see the worry: the struggle had come to this,

the black upright she had once loved haunting
the room it could never leave. And her piano

was now one of a mute, discordant population
doomed to oldfolks homes, bars, church basements,

poolhalls, funeral parlors—or more mercifully
abandoned on back porches where at least

chickens could nest, or the cat have kittens.
So when she could no longer play well enough

even to teach us, she hired some of the men
to haul out and burn the piano in the field behind

the house. We watched the keys catch, furious, and all
at once, heard in the fire a musiclike relief

when the several tons of tension let go, heat
becoming wind on our faces. We learned that

when true ivory burns the flame is playful,
quick, and green. And in the ash, last lessons:

the clawed brass feet we had never before noticed,
the harp's confusion of wire, and the pedals we'd worn

thin, shaped like quenched-hard tongues—*loud, soft,*
sustain. We waited with her until they were cool enough to touch.

ELEVATOR OPERATOR, DANVILLE, VIRGINIA, 1964

All day she ferried them—almost all
women, all white—as they rose to fall

in strict passage, the gondola close to airlessness,
curfew-dark. She filled the forward corner, perched

on a small, fold-down stool from which she could
reach with ease both the lever and the collapsing

metal lattice of the door. All day she closed
them in like perfumed birds rustling nylons,

shopping bags, purses—and released them again
to the few destinations she had to repeat, announcing:

third floor—men's wear, mezzanine—unseen steel
cables controlling all of them in endless,

storied looping. Only children saw her until
most learned not to, looking up instead to the dial

above the door, its face an eclipsed compass,
the ornate brass needle of her voice

sweeping east to west to east by the northern
route—as though the south were never there.

FINGER OF MERCURY

She said we were the usual ones to ask,
despite our mothers' hushing, and wished

she had a better story to tell. But truth
was, she'd been hot one late afternoon,

the sun bare in a cloudless sky, and the pool was closed,
surrounded by a chain-link fence she climbed

with ease. But when she dropped to the other side,
the little finger from her left hand refused,

gravity delivering her of it
with only the slightest resistance.

She felt betrayed when she looked up, saw it
hanging there, lost easily as a tooth,

or a skink's tail. There was no pain at first,
numb blood, and what else was there to do but

climb back up and get it? She drove herself
to the clinic, finger tissue-swaddled, mute infant

too small to save—two joints, a ragged nail,
the whorl of print already failing

evidence of her. The surgeon couldn't
reattach it, but neatened the wound,

fashioning a small, pale flap like an envelope's.
So she placed it in a matchbox and buried it

in the garden next to the cat, telling herself
she wouldn't miss the finger half as much.

And yet her body insisted ever since
on recalling it—with phantom itch, the ache of arthritis

in the bone so real she could, even now, wake
in the morning surprised to find it gone—good

reminder, she said, that she could suffer worse,
a blessing, really, any lesson in smaller loss.

PHOTOGRAPHER

It began with the first baby, the house
disappearing threshold by threshold, rooms

milky above the floor only her heel,
the ball of her foot perceived. The one thing real

was the crying; it had a low ceiling
she ducked beneath—but unscalable walls.

Then she found with the second child
a safer room in the *camera obscura*, handheld,

her eye to them a petaled aperture,
her voice inside the dark cloth muffled

as when they first learned it. Here, too, she steadied,
stilled them in black and white, grayscaled the bee-stung

eye, the urine-wet bedsheet, vomit, pox,
pout, fever, measles, stitches fresh-black,

bloody nose—the expected shared mishap
and redundant disease. In the evenings

while they slept, she developed the day's film
or printed in the quiet darkroom, their images

under the enlarger, awash in the stop bath,
or hanging from the line to dry. Sometimes

she manipulated their nakedness, blonde hair
and bodies dodged whiter in a mountain stream

she burned dark, thick as crude oil or tar. The children's
expressions fixed in remedial reversals,

she sleeved and cataloged them, her desire,
after all, not so different from any other mother's.

AT THE ROUTE ONE FLEA MARKET

Inside makeshift stalls, hawkers slumped in
resigned habit, their tables weighted down

with everything broken—fans, dolls, blenders,
clocks—all destined for the trash heap, suspended—

spared—for at least one more late Saturday afternoon.
To the side and behind them, a lone structure

listed, small as a bedroom—or a circus wagon
stalled at the edge of a field shrinking

toward it. She was its door, set in the blank
wooden frame, old clearly, swaddled in blankets

mummylike, diminishing inward
as though packed with mud and lichen,

her body given over to that kind of waiting.
Three ragged Xs painted black on a cardboard sign

told what she was selling besides some chipped
dishes and empty picture frames: boxes

of magazines and tapes surrounded her,
crowding the shaded space of the room behind her,

all of it handled, wound and rewound, all
those dated, glossed bodies used past desire. Still,

she'd gesture, call out, when anyone wandered
near: *If there's one thing I can't never keep in here,*

it's them pictures—fingering in her patient
lap the small purse, its emptiness worried soft.

THE MEDICAL VENUS

The so-called Mediceische Venus is one of a collection of life-sized anatomical wax models from the late eighteenth century. Designed and used for teaching, she was created and is still kept at Museo La Specola in Florence.

1

In the patient, quiet museum, she is exhibited
closed, indehiscent inside a glass casket,

reclining on her back, on hair long as her spine.
Her face is sublime as in the moment

before sleep, or after waking, eyes opening
or just closing, mouth barely parted as though

to draw a breath or speak, fine teeth suggested
behind the lasting red of her lips. A strand

of pearls encircles, defines her nakedness—
a luminescent sheen of shoulders, breasts,

and thighs—such wholeness a molded disremembrance
of what it took to make her, the wax itself

long removed from the hive's hexagonal prisms,
the cooling fan of temporal wings.

2

She is the house with a wall that removes
to a methodical inner progression

past seven layers—from pearls to rosy lungs,
to the great vessels that enter and leave

the heart, to the pelvic inlet where the fetus,
too, can be lifted out, serene, instructive.

3

On their way from sickbed to cemetery,
over two hundred bodies were dissected,

studied for this one rendering—a first
and last communion with sculptor and surgeon

in the bright tension of a shared studio, the curtain
of their flesh parted also in this mute recital.

4

Both fixed and liquescent, this extreme,
uneasy perfection can never forget

itself the way bronze, granite, marble forget;
this demands greater, almost human care—eager

as it is to reject the suspense of exacting form
and return to the possibilities of motion.

late wife
(2005)

NATURAL HISTORY EXHIBITS

I.

Sometimes they used the hoe, or the dull blade
of a shovel, a stick of firewood, sometimes
the handle of the broom. I grew up around
women who would kill any snake, never
mind what the men said about moles and mice,
about markings or the shape of the head—
the good ones, harmless. Draping the body over
a low branch, my mother would claim, still breathless
from the killing, *rain, this will bring rain.*

II.

In this city's museum, beyond the rooms
of taxidermy, past the lit cases
of arrowheads and spearpoints, snakes are kept
in bright glass cells—a whole wall of them, a live
mural glistening, changing—the harmless
by the deadly. I recognize without
reading the sign the black rat snake; I know
already that it kills not by sudden
poison but wraps itself instead around
its prey, then tightens that embrace until it feels
the fear leave with the struggle, then the breath—
until the constricted heart grows still.

III.

It had to have come up from the cool underbelly
of the first old house we rented, climbing
pipes like branches to make a nest of the rusty
sink-cabinet drawer where I kept the silverware.
I opened it, and the snake lay coiled, brooding
on its bed of edges—blades and tines—

the hard bone handles, a wedding gift
from my mother's aunt. The snake never
raised its head. I hesitated, then
eased shut the drawer. Later, I would wash
every fork, spoon, and knife—and set the table.

IV.

I know now I should have killed the snake
and hung its long body as straight in death
as the glistening barrel of a gun. I was young,
new in my marriage-bed, but regret was already
sunk sharp in me. Like any blade, it would grow
dull slowly. The wound would heal around it
until its absence would cause the greater pain.
A good story, though, how I let the snake
escape, drain back into the house, and for years
I told at that same table what I had to tell,
how it disappeared the way it came.

PHOTOGRAPH: FARM AUCTION

I have only one of the many
    images I watched you make
        out of your vigilant silence.

I am in it. You were documenting
    closure, you would tell me, one
        of many—the death of the small farm,

the small town, the way we had
    grown up there. In the hothouse
        of this frame, I have my back to you,

my arm around my mother's grief;
    the ribs of the umbrella are showing,
        sharp with rain. The auctioneer

points away from us, from you,
    as though sighting with relief the shore,
        his mouth paused beneath the loudspeaker—

a quenched, open morning glory,
    gunmetal hard. When you brought the image
        and this moment from their latency,

you called me into the darkroom
    to see what I had forgotten. You must
        remember how I admired the detail

of a hayfork lying flat in the foreground,
    angling toward the camera you had
        trained on it so that the many tines

are distorted, longer than they could
    have been—like a plate of baleen
        from the mouth of a whale, its rich body

harvested for something this small.

RENT

There were five houses over twenty years.
        We lived almost a decade in one,
                a mild, shallow winter in another.

We bartered work for rent in the last, the one
        that had already been let go. Privet crowded
                the porch, and a wall bowed into the parlor—abandoned

honey swollen inside it, the plaster crazed.
        We would share that house with swallows
                in the chimney, with the black rat snake

I'd find coiled in a basket of clothes,
        or stretched out on the bed. Bumblebees
                purred as though with contentment under us

and spiders—seasonless—survived the broom
        to live in every corner, their egg sacs hung
                like soft, spun pearls. Every spring, the bedroom

filled with termites flying, having come up
        from beneath the floor to mate and shed the brief
                wings I swept up like confetti; committed,

they returned to a narrowing crawlspace
        to feed their queen. I imagined her pale and thick
                as my thumb, invalid, being fed the house,

birthing more of what would keep her fed.
        When I worried the place would fall, you laughed
                not in our lifetime. That was true. It stood

those years where it yet stands, where you remained
        without me, living, you would claim,
                another, finer life, nothing the same.

But I imagine the walls still disappear inside
themselves, vacant forms, and the house grows
lighter, a deceitful ruin that lingers, rising

longer than it should above you and the fertile
hunger that will, with enough time, consume it—
before going on to another survival.

WAXWING

The cedar waxwing had to have
    fallen from some nest you couldn't
        see, so you brought it into the house

to save it. We fed it crickets
    sold boxed for bass bait, kept it in
        the cage we made of the kitchen—

where the bird sat on the sideboard
    for days—its mouth an insatiable,
        urgent flower—before finding flight,

the stalled blade of the ceiling fan,
    other rooms. For weeks we lived
        with the sound of wings. I grew

accustomed to the billing-purr,
    the feel of an electric, furious
        lightness clinging to my shoulder—

what it should have feared. The waxwing
    accepted us as given, and with us
        our seized, repressive sky, glassed light,

narrow stairway. So when we let it go,
    when it refused the atavistic
        sky, remained instead for one full

month in the hickory tree that loomed
    over the house, I asked you why
        we'd fed it. What had we saved

for a world so alien, the waxwing
    must have believed it had died in those rooms
        where for a while we went on living?

EIGHT BALL

It was fifty cents a game
        beneath exhausted ceiling fans,

the smoke's old spiral. Hooded lights
        burned distant, dull. I was tired, but you

insisted on one more, so I chalked
        the cue—the bored blue—broke, scratched.

It was always possible
        for you to run the table, leave me

nothing. But I recall the easy
        shot you missed, and then the way

we both studied, circling—keeping
        what you had left me between us.

PITCHING HORSESHOES

Some of your buddies might come around
for a couple of beers and a game,
but most evenings, you pitched horseshoes

alone. I washed up the dishes
or watered the garden to the thudding
sound of the horseshoe in the pit,

or the practiced ring of metal
against metal, after the silent
arc—end over end. That last

summer, you played a seamless, unscored
game against yourself. Or night
falling. Or coming in the house.

You were good at it. From the porch
I watched you become shadowless,
then featureless, until I knew

you couldn't see either, and still
the dusk rang out, your aim that easy;
between the iron stakes you had driven

into the hard earth yourself, you paced
back and forth as if there were a decision
to make, and you were the one to make it.

POSSESSIONS

I sent you a list of what I wanted, and you boxed it up carelessly,
 as though for the backs of strangers, or for the fire, the way
 you might

have handled a dead woman's possessions—when you could no
 longer bear to touch them, the clothes still fragrant, worn,
 still that reminiscent

of the body. Or perhaps your lover packed the many boxes herself,
 released from secret into fury, that sick of the scent of me

in the bed, that wary of her face caught in my mirror—a thing I
 said then I didn't want, where I would not see myself again.

THE SPANISH LOVER

There were warnings: he had, at forty, never
married; he was too close to his mother,
calling her by her given name, *Manuela,*
ah, Manuela—like a lover; even her face

had bled, even the walls, giving birth to him;
she still had saved all of his baby teeth
except the one he had yet to lose, a small
eyetooth embedded, stubborn in the gum.

I would eat an artichoke down to its heart,
then feed the heart to him. It was enough
that he was not you—and utterly foreign,
related to no one. So it was not love.

So it ended badly, but to some relief.
I was again alone in my bed, but not
invisible as I had been to you—
and I had learned that when I drank sherry

I was drinking a chalk-white landscape, a distant
poor soil; that such vines have to suffer; and that
champagne can be kept effervescent by putting
a knife in the open mouth of the bottle.

THE CHANGE

My mother fought the house as if to rid
herself of it, spring cleaning without regard
for the season. She could drag the awkward bed
to the other side of the room and still have
strength enough to force the wardrobe out
so she could wash the wall behind it, its dark-

carved feet those of a raptor, its shelves layered
with linens embroidered in tight stitches,
her initials like scars risen pale in the healing.
And in the midst of all the scouring—beds stripped,
curtains down—she might at any moment
fling open the window as if to jump from it,

or fly. I understand now how she burned,
and some of why she rearranged those rooms,
so that she might wake and for once be surprised,
disoriented in that place as she was then
in her own body. In this way she fought the change,
her resolve as inextinguishable as the walls'.

SECOND BEARING, 1919

for my father

I have asked him to tell it—how
he heard the curing barn took hours

to burn, the logs thick, accustomed
to heat—how, even when it was clear all

was lost, the barn and the tobacco
fields within it, they threw water

instead on the nearby peach tree,
intent on saving something, sure,

though, the heat had killed it, the bark
charred black. But in late fall, the tree

broke into bloom, perhaps having
misunderstood the fire to be

some brief, backward winter. Blossoms
whitened, opened. Peaches appeared

against the season—an answer,
an argument. Word carried. People

claimed the fruit was sweeter for being
out of time. They rode miles to see it.

He remembers my grandfather
saying, his mouth full, *this is*

a sign, and the one my father
was given to eat—the down the same,

soft as any other, inside
the color of cream, juice clear

as water, but *wait, wait;* he holds
        his cupped hand up as though for me

to see again there is no seed,
        no pit to come to—that it is

infertile, and endless somehow.

THE AUDUBON COLLECTION

The mockingbird, great white heron
        and screech owl hunt, mate, open

their mouths to scream; and the passenger
        pigeon is not extinct in this

framed, collective afterlife: Audubon
        was glass—invisible, exact

as God—into which they flew
        to be studied, perfected, to hang

on the walls of my house. He preferred
        to work from the dead; the certain

stillness afforded the intimacy necessary
        for this much detail, the captured-

alive too resigned or terrified,
        the preserved too perfect a lie.

(As a young man he'd been
        commissioned to make a portrait

of a child disinterred, and he had
        drawn a live likeness; even then

he could see beyond the mask.)
        He had to work quickly—often

drawing all night before the colors
        of the eyes and talons could fade, before

the advancing rigor. Dissecting some
        so that he might see what they'd eaten,

he sometimes cooked and ate one, declaring
    the herring gull "salty," the starling

"delicate." He killed countless
    for these portraits, his desire that precise,

that exhaustive. There will always be
    such things I regret knowing.

Still, in the margin before daybreak,
    when the darkness is unchanged,

but any chance of sleep lost,
    I can wake to their voices restored,

transfigured to one, distinctive, clear,
    but bodiless—in spite of everything,

rendered unrecognizable, beyond
    the walls—the window glass calling out

of something like despair, or hope,
    somewhere in the flightless trees.

THE PRACTICE CAGE

I was taking my routine run, the same
three miles just past daybreak on the jogging trail
that encircled the playing fields—the home

of the Fighting Eagles. I'd run that course
so many times I imagined myself
a goat circling the invisible stake

of the baseball diamond's off-season
desolation, scoreboard blank before
the lightening sky. Behind the stands, I heard

first the dozen crows that crowded around
a practice batting cage—a metal-framed,
room-sized rectangle, its sides and ceiling

made of a thick, heavy net. Then I saw
the cause of the complaint: a red-tailed hawk
on the ground inside. I'd spent most of my life

in the country before moving to this city.
I'd seen hundreds of hawks, but what I knew
of them was distant patience, or an extreme,

diving speed, or death. I walked toward
the cage, and the crows rose, scattered. The hawk
flew up into the corner, struggled there,

twisting upside down as though tearing
this other sky with his talons, before
going limp, still turned, wings splayed outward.

Where I expected tension, fury, I saw
instead the taming of despair—his eyes
resigned to this, to me, softened somehow

as though with forgiveness. I could see where
he'd flown in, one edge of the netting gapped,
so I worked the knots to raise the hem

higher while the bird hung, indifferent
to my effort, so motionless I was
certain he was injured by the struggle.

But when I spoke, urged him, tugged at the net
below, he seamlessly let go from that
stillness, dropped down and righted himself into flight,

finding at once the wider gap—and was,
with no wingbeat at all, gone, clearing the lip
of the stadium to disappear into the turning

stand of poplars bordering the fields.
I began my run again then, elated
by the sound of my own breathing, by my feet

striking the ground beneath me, by knowing
I would round that same turn, time after
time, to see again in that familiar emptiness

something we had revised, an absence finished.

ATLAS

In the museum gift shop at the foot
of Marye's Heights, a lone, slim volume
entitled *Orthopaedic Injuries*

of the Civil War lay remaindered
at half price, a book many
had handled without wanting to

own. I could not resist, either,
looking inside, compelled by two
photographs, portraits on the cover

of the same formal young man:
in one image, both of his legs
are missing; in the other, he wears

prosthetic limbs, bared for the camera.
In image after image, the book
catalogs particular survivals,

organized by the anatomic
regions of loss: *extremities,*
upper and lower, thigh, shoulder—;

some men are halved and in the next
photograph risen from ether
or chloroform, from opium

and whiskey, to wear inventions
of wood, leather, metal. They had
survived the bullet, the surgeon's knife,

and now this first, rough reconstruction
of the body, to look past the aperture
and into the photographer, wearing

the century's dark caul, then into me.
    I bought the book, but not for their
        unique disfigurements; it was

their shared expression I wanted—resolve
    so sharply formed I cannot believe
        they ever met another death.

ARTIFACT

For three years you lived in your house
just as it was before she died: your wedding
portrait on the mantel, her clothes hanging
in the closet, her hair still in the brush.
You have told me you gave it all away
then, sold the house, keeping only the confirmation
cross she wore, her name in cursive chased
on the gold underside, your ring in the same

box, those photographs you still avoid,
and the quilt you spread on your borrowed bed—
small things. Months after we met, you told me she had
made it, after we had slept already beneath its loft
and thinning, raveled pattern, as though beneath
her shadow, moving with us, that dark, that soft.

POND TURTLE

You want to feed it; we both do. We have
come to know it well by its trailing veil
of air purling the water. This doesn't school,
and fish scatter before it. The massive
body just beneath the surface, it moves
the way your eye moves beneath a translucent
lid of dream. All is defense: the mud-
covered shell, the ragged blade of the mouth,

the head thicker than your clenched fist. Breaking
through my reflection, it displaces me as it feeds
on what we have cast here. It takes no pleasure
I can see; that is for us. Instead, it suffers our care
for it—and is perhaps relieved when the bread
is gone and when we can no longer see the breathing.

THE COUGH

You can't recall when it first appeared in her,
but it must have been in late summer,
around the time the locusts came and muted
crickets, birdsong, the wind. And in the same way you
would not have perceived a tightening in the trees
before the onslaught of that sound, you noticed nothing
before it—fatigue perhaps, intolerance for the heat.
She kept saying then that it would pass with the season,

insisted, even as it consumed her, grew
bolder, not sleeping even when she slept.
It would outlive the locusts, but by days few
enough to count—the translucent forms still left
clinging to the world they had overset,
each one a perfect mold of the body that refused it.

DRIVING GLOVE

I was unloading groceries from the trunk
of what had been her car, when the glove floated
up from underneath the shifting junk—
a crippled umbrella, the jack, ragged
maps. I knew it was not one of yours,
this more delicate, soft, made from the hide
of a kid or lamb. It still remembered
her hand, the creases where her fingers

had bent to hold the wheel, the turn
of her palm, smaller than mine. There was
nothing else to do but return it—
let it drift, sink, slow as a leaf through water
to rest on the bottom where I have not
forgotten it remains—persistent in its loss.

FURNACE

Just moved, we were still living out of boxes
when the old furnace refused another winter,
filling the house with oily smoke that woke us,
breathless. It would take them an entire
day to dismember and carry it up—
while the radiators' cold ribs rang, shuddered
with the sawing. All afternoon the deep
laughter of those rough surgeons rose up

from beneath the floor, the house grown rigid
with cold, while the blackened parts—dust flue and ashpit—
were piled on the street to be hauled off. The rooms
again would swell with heat, the house given
back to itself, ignorant of this warmth's new origin,
immune again, as we would never be, to the season.

STRINGED INSTRUMENT COLLECTION

You began it the third fall you were alone,
and soon they surrounded you: mandolins,
mandolas, guitars—cutaways, dreadnoughts—
the upright bass. You spent most of those nights
with the jazz guitar, learning Birdland and Twilight Time.
The others hung from inlaid necks, scrolled heads,
patient, mute, the way they hang now from
these walls. You claim no wood is ever dead,

even if it's gone to fire and risen as heat,
and think of them not as possessions but as guests
who will survive you, pass to other hands
the way they passed to yours. Sometimes a name
called out, a cough, a laugh will echo here—our voices
in the hollows of their bodies, for now, sustained.

BUYING THE PAINTED TURTLE

Two boys, not quite men, pretended to let it go
only to catch it again and again. And the turtle,
equally determined, each time gave
its heart to escape them. We were near
the base of the old dam where the river
became a translucent, hissing wall, fixed
in falling, where, by the size of it, the turtle
had long trusted its defense, the streaming

algae, green, black, red—the garden of its spine—
not to fail it. They held it upside down,
the yellow plastron exposed; they hoisted it
over their heads like a trophy. I left it
to you to do the bargaining, exchange
the money for us to save it, let it go;

fast, it disappeared into deeper
water, returning to another present,
where the boulders cut the current to cast
safer shadows of motionlessness. We were
already forgotten, then, like most gods
after floods recede, after fevers break.

We did not talk about what we had bought—
an hour, an afternoon, a later death,
worth whatever we had to give for it.

pinion
(2002)

ASUNDER

The field before us lay fallow, clover-
bruised and healing, a crop we would plow under.
The plant-bed bandaged what lay just beyond
the willows; I could see it white and clean
through the trees. Mother screamed again,
and I knew by now the women in her room
must be wading in blood. That scream raveled
and lashed Father, whose eyes lay on that fallow
field guiltless as a hawk's, who was himself
so tired evenings he could not speak,
but who climbed those stairs to her, and broke her.

We were all gotten in that raw silence
and came to be with measured vengeance.
I can still see him, resolute, between
the spread legs of a plow, and know how
he looked getting me.
                                        But now I was
old enough to have my own son.
                                                            "You," I did not say,
"you don't remember the time a hen nested
in the dead belly of that apple tree:
a winged tumor Mother said leave be
or I'd lose an eye. I waited till she was
not brooding, and I plumbed what had gone
from rot to hollow, was sunk up to my shoulder
when she bore down on me; I learned the sound
of myself with wings. Mother beat me, too,
the shell breaking, the yolk bleeding from my fist.
I defied her. I stood up and sucked
my thumb; from my second finger, and my third,
sucked what might have left this place, what might
have hatched in the belly of that tree.
On the seat of my pants I wiped a wild
generation.

'You are your father,' she said,
'you are your father all over again.'"

No. There would be no more voices born
thin as if with mourning.
"If you touch her
again, I'll kill you," I said as the midwife leaned
out the window, called down a girl. His shoulders
swayed, gave in.
"Don't you even go up
there. You go on up to the barn and sleep.
You can listen to the hogs rut. Maybe
that will soothe you."
"Before we were married,"
he answered me, "I used to brush her hair
for her; it was long and cool and deep
and I could not get close enough. Look at you.
You are the measure of it."

CURING TIME

I was all day in a black, ordered heat
so thick and still and sweet I vomited
into tiered darkness. And still the task
fell to me to keep the barn's fires going
all night. If I slept, I dreamed myself swung high,
scorching, strung by my wrists, fists numb.
Awake,
I burned on my cot; I lay there, twisting
tobacco leaves into spirals so tight
they doubled back onto themselves, looped, knotted.
My fists appeared, disappeared, in the rising
light of a wasted moon.
Sister's breasts waxed
against it; she was that familiar to me.
There used to be no tide in her. I feared
this changeling who strung bright leaves, her hands
quick and flying. I straddled the beams high
in the swollen gut of the barn, and her laughter
beat past the low rectangle of light—a swallow,
it sought this hollow dusk. Later, straddling
the mule, I knew her laugh in the soundless
distance by her head thrown back, her mouth
filled with sky. She rang the dull bell; it rhymed
itself, calling me to heavy meals,
my tongue dead in my mouth. The water
she hauled boiled against the lip of the dipper.
I could not drink enough. She was fractured
as the moon was by cycles of light.
My fists
appeared, disappeared, in rising light
beside a barn that bore in the chinking
the handprints of another generation:
the lone, crooked thumb, here a splay of fingers,
the heel and palm. I turned to wrench the dark,
cured leaves, my hands the hands of a stranger.

THE PROOF-METER

All those years the mule's tail swung a ragged
rhythm I likened to the beat of a lone
black wing, loftless, dogged. He could measure
a row perfect, but he could balk and squat,
too, and smile at me. I wanted a machine—
gleaming and blind—that I could finally ride,
that would not sicken, that would not lift its tail
and shit, that would never founder. The mule,
unharnessed, drowsed in the pasture, lowering
his head to random grazing, lifting it
to watch with disinterest his replacement,
sterile as well, and so no kin. I learned
the gauges—the gas and oil, temperature—
and found the proof-meter that recorded
not miles but time. How did it know there was
no distance here? Only these fields, cedar-
bourne, only this creek, rising and sagging
in its bed. The dusk, half-caste, hung on
as the greased, stubborn piston-beat doused
the locusts. The high-beam cut the falling
weight of that night, and darkness foundered on
its one wing. The mule, proving nothing, swung
his sluggish tail, beat out his one known hour.

PINION

I was dragging up the trunk of a wet
red oak when it hung a stump, and I lost
purchase; the tractor reared and fell
back on me. I was held fast there, pinioned, not
dying, growing numb and light, wait-crazed
and finally calm. The creekbank saved me;
its wet reasoned it would take me back, gave
every time I took a breath. I breathed
down; my chest did not rise; my spine fell
into that wet depression, and a beech
tree wheezed, and the creek strangled itself
on the rocks, and time was severed to bleed
beside me and then clot. Impressed: stone, cartilage,
gristle, bone, muscle, clay. I smelled it;
the woods were ripe with it, and the drone of the locusts
rose, reclaimed my voice, disclaiming me.
A lone crow landed on the tractor tire,
and it turned with him, devolving. He looked
at me and spoke, "Be quick now about it,
before the others hear." And as he spun
slowly, the mud fell from that wheel, meat
from its bone, and the crow growled, his mouth
shut. I saw the paling stalks then; with a dream-eye,
open in that feathered belly, I saw the dead
silk, the sweet milk seep from the abundance
I had thought mine. I watched the wind thresh
the fluming leaves of tobacco, the bright glut
of morning glories. The bottomland bore
old freshet scars, and in the woods, fat stumps
oozed my story. And then I was over
a strange country I knew nothing of.
In the meantime a spider had come; from
her distended belly the line raveled,
a fine, umbilical self enjambed, her web

definite in the steering wheel. By a clean
incision, a locust had left itself,
hollow but clinging to my shirt. A kingfisher
had flown down with the dusk to eat where the water
had worried a ragged, blank margin.
Soon they would come find me and interrupt it,
but not before I saw the way things are,
not before I saw, cast from the belly
of that halcyon, its confession
of ribs, a conversion fallen clean and white,
indefinite, on the creekbank's placid sand.

FINE AS SILK

March 1924, warm, fine

The boys would only sop it in their gravy,
talk, if they did talk, with their mouths full
of it. But in the hour the sourdough rose,
I sat in the kitchen doorway and watched the guineas
abandon me to fuss and settle with dusk
in the trees. Mother faint again in the room
above, I listened, heard only the yeast
murmur in its bowl a cold and lazy boil.
I rolled up my sleeves and floured my hands
to punch it down, what was risen pale and full
as her belly swelling even now, the house
heavy with grown men. It would be mine
to raise as they were not, though their mouths
were mine to fill, their beds mine to change,
the red field-mud they tracked into the house,
mine.

The guineas had hidden their heads beneath
their wings; they blinded themselves as I dusted
the kneading bowl with flour sifted fine as silk, and so
I disappeared as I sank my fists into it.

HER HEART'S CREAM

April 1924, mild, windy

I

How could Mother ever have mistaken it
for the Change. Never mind the eighteen years
beneath which she had lain, a field he had
let go, let grow up in whatever whim
volunteered itself: broomsedge, groundbriars,
saplings in rows grown dull, edgeless. Hoarfrost
turned it, churned up stones. And as a field
goes back to no purpose, she had reclaimed
herself, his hands no more to her than a disheveling
wind that can only go so deep, his desire
no more than a hawk borne on that wind.
                                                            She knew,
though, as she knew when she hung the bedsheets
on the line, the wind would seek them out, wallow
in the sluggish damp until they were
dry and quick with it—as she had before
known blood to go to bone inside her, known
two hearts to beat, as she had held another tongue.

II

Every last newborn I had seen come quick
or dead into this world had come finished
in a slick and glistening caul iridescent
as a snail's slow wake but blood-coursed—the kittens
in the pantry's dark, the still fall calf
steaming in the stall. And still I could
not reconcile all that with what now bound
Mother to her bed, her breath rapid
and shallow as the panicked wingbeat of a bird
trapped in a nervous room as it fought against
the wall's stricture, the lie the windows told,

swore to. I thought surely it would escape her,
fly from between her lips like some hard-kept
truth and leave this room, the house, the land,
leave be this woman who gave her daughter
all that rose up sweet in her, her heart's cream.
Every evening, she brushed and braided, telling
how she, too, had been able to sit
on her hair, showing me the thick braid saved
in tissue paper, where it lay coiled
in odd detachment, twin in heft and measure
to mine, where it yet held its oblivious sheen.

THE ADMIRER

September 1926, clear

He had before come courting—with pecans
or peaches, berries. I had those times been able
to thank him with one of my pies and be
done with him. For this, though, he would want
supper, to sit at the table with me
after supper. For this, I reckoned he had
spent most of the morning emptying
the sky of its plenty: the doves spilled from
burlap in iridescent disarray,
three dozen at least, a shimmering

bouquet. And so the afternoon was for me
defined; the hour deepened the mound of feathers,
blue-gray, plucked in porch-dusk, and the wind,
disinterested, would once in a while stir them.
I knew they were easy to bring down
over a field where they would fall into
the tangled grasses and go on flying against
what had been wind. Easy—as this was not:
feet, gut, heart, the smooth brow with eyes open
like garnets glowing; I cut and tossed over

and over what was in the end useless
onto the feathers, a last and bloody bed,
or to the cats, who growled and circled me,
to keep the peace. A dove would amount to,
at best, a half-dozen mouthfuls, the dark
breast tender but gristled with shot—black seed.
I threw a whole bird to the nursing cat
and wondered whether the white kitten had opened
its eyes; if they were blue, it would be deaf,
I had been told, and told I could not let it

live. I would see about that. Mother called down,
"How are they coming?" More work than they're worth,
I answered her, for such a little meat.
Even with the birds still baking, yet to be
eaten, with still the biscuits to stir up
and gravy yet to make from the meager fat—
with a strait hour to pass before he would
lean back from the table to pick his teeth and sigh—
I had decided he should have left the doves
their beloved sky, for I would not be won.

BATHING MOTHER

Late May 1927, hot

The cough came and never left, became
a thing unto itself, possessed her throat,
her lungs, the way a whippoorwill consumes
a tree with its convulsive call, willful,
grief-fed. Nothing calmed it, and the season
did not make it any easier:
the fields steamed, tobacco sown in humid
stitches; pollen hung thick as smoke, swollen
on the bees' legs—heavy, sulfur-colored—
as they weaved into the sickroom, and out
again, as though drunk on the fertile world,
its bright contagion.
Even now, I found
her beautiful, and kept her so, combing
her hair away from her damp brow as the house
below complained, grumbled, an empty belly
I let go without. I sang to her; I read;
I bathed the mother of us all, my hands
dark swallows flying close over the surface
of a pond—whose depths churned, unimaginable—
to make it still, until it was so.

THRESHOLD

Mother's wake, September 1927, cooler

I washed and dressed you, stroked the smooth inner
cool of your wrist, the place where the pulse had lain,

but you remained formless. The house was filled
with the whispers of neighborwomen, the smell

of cooking. I knew we must feed the mouths
of the living. You had taught me that. Now

I crossed your hands beneath your breasts; you looked
prepared for a journey, preoccupied

with the going. But you would not know anything
of a journey; your eyes were closed against

the way he had cut to this place, the strait
road you once told me you saw as a neat

seam or the familiar scar of a deliberate
cut, the kind a surgeon would make and admire,

pride himself on. No, you would know nothing
of going. And then I saw, instead of a coffin,

a narrow, deeper doorway; in it you posed, still,
completed by the frame, the lintel and sill

of cedar. You balanced on the threshold
of this moment, of the absolute.

I imagined you standing in that entrance,
behind you the house, room after sentient

room, behind you a wake of patient clay
and granite, a shifting shelf of ash and slate—

the biding center of the earth your parlor.
You would not ask me in, though it would be years

before you shut the door and backed into it.

BAITING THE TRAP

This was Nate's lazy living: His guile finer
than theirs, they fell for easy meat in the yawn
of tense, metallic jaws. I walked that line
only once with him; that was enough
to see what struggled in the trap, enough
to watch Nate stand on the pelt to save it
from blemish. I felt that growling through the soles
of my boots. I felt my own bones hum. And for what,
I asked, and he said, "A woman's tired desire
to swaddle herself in something soft and wild."
"Man has no advantage over the beasts," I said;
he wrenched open that jaw, disputed me.
Then he reversed her on a board, and her inner
skin showed white—exposing no secret
after all—already something unto itself,
cleansed against what lay now in the dust and drew
fat, black flies. "For the fate of the sons of men
and the fate of beasts is the same." And he answered,
"This is the only resurrection."
He could not
frighten me then because I believed he was
lost. I waited past the yammering dusk;
I watched his shadow wash up. Around me
heavy sloes hung, clotted. Their bitter
seeds—bones in the womb—I crushed between my teeth.
I watched the wind-flayed willow braid, unbraid,
longing for an admirer, a looking glass.
I ran my tongue in one sweet hull, in the bruised,
immanent void I could not swallow. I
would go in and sit at the supper table
with him, but not before I saw a star
falling burn past its sudden unbecoming—
its fast, evanescent scar—to what stays.

CAUL

My hand floated before me, the scored palm
pale, disfamiliar. It beckoned me. Thirst
grew like a gourd, a swollen void. I had
seen the moon fall into a well and float
there, while it hung, umbra and bone, above.
I had placed my lips against my lips
and drunk myself. And still I lay on the water.
I drew up the sheet to cover my face
against the heat. I saw the window as I
first saw it, through a caul, breathless.

HOARFROST

A pale rime survived the night in long cedar-
shadows I broke beneath my feet. The field
had lost its voice; cut, dried, spiraled, and baled,
it saved itself for winter, for this retelling:
I had delivered a dead calf with a rope
and a come-along. I had pulled the headstone
the same way from the suck of its grave.
With my knife I had dug mud from the serifs
of my own name. In those days there were things
worth saving: the womb for the fall calf,
the name a bridegroom would give. So I
worked the wind-tense fields and waited—turned
again and again the mirror's crazed face
to the wall—and still, I would turn under
the hay-balk and open the field for seed.

CURING TIME

Stringing—August 1928, hot and humid

My muslin shift clung to me, wet and close
as the mist that had been burned off the creek's back
an hour ago. The ground-pulling was done,
and the heavy dew gone from the leaves yet
to be pulled. The mule plodded up and past me,
stopped where he had stopped before, and would again.
He wore blinders and so would not meet my
eye. Blinded from what, I wondered, the strait
sameness of the field's rows, this easy maze?

If he could see in full that endless grid
he might rouse himself from his standing sleep
to rear frothing against it. His head bowed,
he swung his tail instead, and black flies rose
in an angry sigh from the shimmering
blond mirage of his flesh.
                                        Rose appeared
holding a tobacco worm, bloated-green,
and waited for me to watch while she
pulled off its head—the head of a prophet

hard-sought, hated, but much-heeded. She got
a penny for every one she killed,
and we had yet to see this season what
the thing foretold—itself with wings. It wanted,
I supposed, only what I wanted,
to love this given lot, to take this fickle
plenty as wished for, and live long enough
to crawl wet from the womb that was my body,
claiming the wind above the field as much

as I did claim the field, finding that low,
familiar sky far enough to go.
And all the while my hands flew before me,
could well have been any one woman's

as I strung the leaves, hand after hand,
for the boys to hoist whole acres into
the hot, hermetic night of the curing barn.
Even in a hundred years, when the brighter heavens
would be pulled down inside that one room, when it

would have given way to the slow cajole of poison
ivy, honeysuckle, sumac, when the wind
would enter what had been made tight against it,
this place would yet smell of a heat ordered,
measured to *fix* and *dry* and *scorch;* its breath
would still be mine, its sanctuary ever
night in its former world. The string passed through
my hands, and it was as though a mile lapsed,
then another; the line would not be

measured any other way. All those miles,
raveled, saved like odd buttons, scrap cloth,
soap slivers, pins, that image of myself
in the spooled distance. From there, I might believe
it finished once and for all, the crop made
in spite of the field's griefs: sun, drought, sucker, worm, and mold.
In spite of this, I would see it cured at last,
stripped clean of all the hail had left, naked stalks
strict witness to what I had devoured: all

these hours unmeasured as one. A crow
dropped from the sky to stroll, a frocked preacher
among the damsons, already falling,
and like a preacher panted, lusty here
in the midst of this much loss. The cows
stood marble-like, the color of headstones—
and in their slow schooling crowded the shade to carve
the hard salt-block with stubborn tongues: *To live
in hearts we leave behind is not to die.*

GLOVE

Late August 1928, cloudy

I

All afternoon as I snapped beans, as my lap
filled with the sound of a man's knuckles cracking,
she flew about me. I liked to imagine
it was the same wren, come year after year
to the back porch, who chose to nest here
amidst the mess the boys created. She found
in it a wealth of hollows. One time she chose
a swinging gourd, one year a boot, and though
the boys fussed, I would not allow them to disturb
her. Last year, she finally decided
on a can of rusty nails that had fallen
over, and she built on the frozen spill.

She never chose well, and this was even
more precarious: on the narrow
shelf behind me, a lone work glove—molded
open, like the bronzed cast of a hand—cupped
the emptiness she claimed.

Once, in the dusk
of the root cellar, I shuffled heavy jars
of beets, peach halves, snaps, tomatoes. Nothing
looked good in that light. The jars I had yet to fill
lined the bottom shelf, and a shadow in one
drew me down. What drew a mouse into that
empty black mouth? Once there, how long did it pedal
against smooth, invisible walls in full
sight of all it had left behind, of all
it could not reenter? The skeleton reminded
me of a ship in a bottle, sails furled, its ribs
a fragile hull, the skull a socketed prow,
bound to take on nothing as it cut a static sea.

II

At first, the wren stole close by: from the abandoned
web of a spider, from the broom. Then she left
me for lichen, moss, a long, coarse hair
from the mule's tail. She worked, ecstatic;
in her mouth, she carried the earth, though she would
lay her eggs where the palm's salty ache had been.

We worked on. Beyond us, a hawk fell
like a blade into the field where the cow
rubbed her broad, whorled forehead against the knot
on a cedar. That shadow the dead persimmon
tree cast on the chimney darkened until
it was again a scar—or, no, the wound
itself—or any fissured reverie
into which I could fall. And when night closed
it, the seam would take me with it.
                                                            Sometimes I felt
as though I put up food for a great flood,
that I filled the hull and waited for a certain
rain, or perhaps that flood had long come
and frozen, invisible, the world beyond
sunken, the ghost town with it—and now I
waited, icebound, for the day when the bird
would not return, when she would instead
disinherit the habit of this place.

THE DEER

October 1928, summer-like

I had known the dog before in fall to bring
up a foreleg with its black hoof—delicate,
new, shined as patent leather—or the spine
still wearing its remnant of hide. This day
he came, heavy-footed and gaunt, onto
the porch bearing only the deer's lower
jaw that held still its neat teeth in the V
the body had followed in a bounding
wake. I had known geese to leave in that same
shape, the first bird threading some invisible
needle while below it I let down the hem
of Rose's dresses, severing the thread
with my teeth, or quilted down the sky,
pieces of flight in my lap.
                                        The jawbone
lay time-scoured, a clean offering. Detached,
it had been what mine was—the cradle
of the tongue—and its last bed. I knew
then I bore in me the form of this slow
migration, the turn to the tropic of bone.

SNOWBOUND, CHRISTMAS

December 1928, blizzard

The almanac predicted it—and now
at noon the birds retreated as at dusk
into the cedar, though the winter wheat still showed
green beneath the snow—light as a veil
of lace—and the field shone copper with broomsedge.
The road burned red for another hour before the world
revised itself and took back the pond, the fenceline.
Trees kneeled before us while we hauled water
for the animals, then for us, while we brought
in the firewood. The water would freeze
in the bucket before dawn—but for now
the kitchen warmed with the hen baking,
and the cat yawned—her tongue, her throat a glozed
coal—before she curled around herself.
And with no hope of company or kin
we breathed, relieved at a sudden joy.
At last, we could not leave. We brought up
the apples we had stored in the cellar,
popped corn dried in the husks. It exploded
into white over the fire while the cradle
of ice stilled all that lay within it. We
lifted the violin from its case, from
its green velvet sleep, and sang then, our shadows
on the walls where they wrestled, strange, gilded
angels, with the portraits' grave faces—those hated
likenesses: *You—you are so like your father.*
The bow droned. We drank the last of Mother's
wine she had made from sloes grown in the frozen
arbor. The fire died down to the voices
of birds, to ash, then to our own voices
singing out as one from the burning tree.

pharaoh, pharaoh

(1997)

SEARCHING THE TITLE

I. *In the courthouse*

My interest in it is curiosity.
It was a generation lost before
my conception. Still, I am close enough
to feel cheated of it; the bitterness
I did inherit with clear title. The loss
begins with what I know, the land's legal
declension from *father, father's* to neighbors' names,
strangers' names, the names of corporations—
a place encumbered, unencumbered, zoned,
divided, fenced against what had been itself.

II. *The map*

The map unscrolls to an old, forgotten dimension.
I see its maker drew a fine compass,
ornate; *North, South, Orient, Levant* fade
before me, fail me. I am lost. And still
I see here what I can, imagine I,
one of its ghosts, wander this displaced
landscape. Yes, here the world is flat, bound where
the river waves its drawn, pale water, where
the pines stand mute, tedious. And here, the gaping
space the maker labeled the Indian Fields—

a void in the middle of all detail, whose acreage
the legend could tell me, exactly, in hundreds—lies
close, whole, beneath the span of one splayed hand,
the palm down that waved itself before me,
before I could command it, limit it,
reduce it to *my*, before it would be read
in its detail: heartline, lifeline, line
of fate, of fortune, the mounts of Jupiter
and Luna; the plain of Mars—cool, dry—lies
against what was grass and wind in grass.

III. *The legend*

The map's legend reminds me of another,
though both reveal the degree to which any truth
can be abstracted. A changeless place,
uncharted, lies beneath those fields—a cave
whose mouth is lost. The old folks used to sigh
and claim it breathed, exhaled one cool breath for days
before it needed another. They said
it knew no season, was only itself—
fixed—a finished darkness that had known fire
before their fire had ever been conceived.

A pineknot hisses, fumes, is swallowed up.
The smallest flame waves massive shadows here,
writhes against this version of the world
where bats with winged hands wring from its darkness
flight, cling to what we fear. Like theirs, my voice
comes back to me, but mine the voice of a stranger
I know I cannot trust. I discover
a cache of quartz confuses light like water.
And then, not painted, but relieved in ocher,
their hands appear before me, dance and wave;

familiar, they calm the darkness in this
deeper cradle, their palms smooth, blank stone.
The way back is lost to dream. I scroll
the map, turn my back on what cannot be mine,
even in memory. What I know, I own:
a murder of crows rises from a broken field
as though from violent seed; a blood-beech seethes
all winter; two hawks spar against the dusk-
marred pines. I don't dispute with them this boundary,
their shared desire for this sky, this spiraled lie:
and so to the point and place of beginning.

AUCTION

Some things bring nothing. Later there will be
a bonfire of palm-worn plow handles.
But a doll, pallid—china hands fractured—
brings fifteen dollars.
                                        His bed they have hauled
out, the covers still on it, an old man's
nest of tangled flannel. I think he has
no daughters to know what must not be
sold. His late wife's dressing table gives up
its confused vanities: snaggletooth combs,
the warbled wire of hairpins, a lipstick,
a faint layer of blush over all. The sun-
shocked mirror denies this face, waves my hair,
widens my eyes, until I cannot see
the resemblance. Is this how she saw
herself? And over her shoulder the fields,
falling away from the house, steep with
distortion? Under her crushed narcissus,
the varicose wake of a mole heaves
as if the vagrant dead—grown bolder—rise,
thick palms bared for this shallow, movable darkness.

AIRSTREAM

My mother's brother comes back one summer in five,
or one summer in seven, to what he does
not call his home. My mother does not blame
him, she claims; *there was nothing here for him.*
There was nothing here. She devils eggs.
She watches. *Mama rocked him till his feet*
dragged the floor, she tells me; *he was twelve years old*
when she died; he was just about your age.

He drives up at dusk, the swifts still spinning
in the last light. He pulls an old Airstream
behind him, and it glows, reflects the motion
of the sky, reflects my face, the faint moon.
I am called to crawl inside my uncle's
mirror, what he has brought from Oklahoma,
what he has brought from home. I have never
seen my mother cry she is so happy.

We are hours on the front porch; his boots
drag, drawl under the swing. The rust-chains
sing above his weight. He tells stories
about tornadoes: how he's seen a broomstraw
driven straight through a lightpole; he's seen a mirror
that was picked up and set back down unbroken
miles away; and once he saw a house
disappear except for a vase of fresh-cut flowers

that marked the plot like a grave. And he is not
afraid, has never been afraid of what
sends the natives down into their shelters
like prairie dogs. They think he's crazy not
to fear the sullen quiet of intense depression,
the horizon sick and jaundiced, the green lightning,
the buildings bursting from the higher pressure
that is trapped within them not unlike mean grief.

The wind comes unappeasable and coils
around itself, around the hollow core
of not-wind and crazed lightning; luminous
within its own dusk—dust-gorged and pulsing—
a hissing, ragged artery bleeds backwards
into itself; without edge, it spirals
what it did not choose of what was in its path,
all it keeps as futile, flawless memory

to be set down miles from home, in a rain of blood,
as the wind, still sinuous, dies again, again.
Imagine that, my mother says, *imagine.*
To her, he looks like one of us. He still
belongs, his forehead high, recognizable,
the way he laughs the same. I swing beside
him, terrified of all that he has seen.
I dream that night the wind flies me miles away

and sets me down so softly I cannot feel
myself. He wants to visit the old homeplace
and so we go with shovel and rake to repair
the graves that are all we own of that slow ruin.
Kudzu pulls the house down on itself
and poison ivy rises from the chimney.
Her grave has settled into a deepening
depression. *He was just about your age.*

He buries her again. Again he feels
that old fear not of any visible abyss
but of this furious, recurring worm—dust-gorged
and pulsing—and its slow, decomposing,
downward suck. What it takes into itself
is not set down except in memory—
what cannot be trusted—or in the slope
of a child's cheek, the angle of the brow—

all that the womb can mirror. He will have
his own wife and child, and less and less
of us. He will live his life where he
can see for miles. My mother cries all day
that day he leaves for home, the Airstream
luminous and rocking in a fog of dust
that picks up and swirls around itself, around
the sudden absence that has become the core.

PORTRAIT

Twenty years' woodsmoke coats the glass
on her gilt-framed portrait,
but the pentimento's roving eye
catches his and is enough
and not even necessary
for him to see the night she cried
to die and he rubbed her back,
the liniment becoming
a molten membrane between his hands
and the bones rising
uprooted and disoriented
as if through still water.

He buried her under the red clover
while the cattle trudged closer,
heads low, chewing, puzzling.
Her milk cow's bell tolled:
This is where I am.

THE MILK COW SPEAKS OF WINTER

He pulls a full moon from my swollen bag;
the warm lunar landscape fogs far away
from me, though his forehead rises and falls
with each breath I take, light against my ribs.
Sometimes he speaks or sings or clucks his tongue,
and I watch him unfold his pocketknife,
sever the twine from another hay bale,
its dust rising with his icy white breath
as the tension collapses, relaxes
at his feet. I am offered last year's field,
and with the grass the rare brittle carcass
of a bird, grim beak hinged closed, the morning
glories smothered with their mouths wide open,
and the hollow bodies of grasshoppers
stunned midleap that morning he's forgotten.
He steals from the field as he steals from me.
I stand for him to curse and wrench the year's
staggering calf; at last I yearn to feel
his fists filling a galvanized bucket
with steady relief. And I lean into
his nuzzle, silent, my tongue the thick wind
that rolls over his chapped winter field,
my teeth sweet with red blossoms of clover.

THE MOON IS MADE

Phil sold cigarettes and soft drinks up front
and poured peach brandy in the back room
of his corner gas station. Summers,
my brother and I would ride our bikes
around the two pumps to ring the bell,
and Phil would yell not to and not mean it.
He sliced rat cheese from a huge wheel, waned
by appetite like a foul yellow moon
flat on its back; in deep July heat
it reeked its gravitational pull.
We bought hunks in white butcher paper
and Saltines for lunch; hunkered down
inside on cool concrete, we listened
to Phil talk dirty about women.
Well, you think, that's all a fine memory,
except that even though I tried to
hide it with high tops and a Cubs cap,
I was a little girl, and I knew
he knew it. But even my big brother
only laughed when Phil rolled back the tin
on kippers and said, "Don't let your nose
stop your tongue every time." And he winked
at me, at what he knew I would be,
then tossed back his head, dropped a headless
fish in his mouth to swim blindly down
while my shame, nameless, soured and curdled,
and the moon fumed and overcame me.

IN THE ACOUSTIC SHADOW

I think she liked to frighten me with it.
The great-aunt held the minié ball in her palm,
a small egg, bone-gray lead, and said, "This is
The Wilderness. This is how close you came
to that common Confederate grave."
I never tired of it or the story
of how this improbable artifact lodged
sixty years in the trench it had burrowed
in her grandfather's temple; how his skull
closed over it easy as a tree heals
around barbed wire, scarred by defiant,
defined not by deformity but pain;
how to remove it would have killed him; how
he feared sharing the grave with it and made
her grandmother swear to have it cut from
his dead body and she did, as if that
could deliver him too late from memory;
how the story of who shot him was told
by its three-ringed base: *a Yankee, at least*
it was a Yankee; how folks passed around
what did not kill him—this dormant tumor;
how it came to rest in her grandmother's
jewelry box, sunk beneath the cameos
and brooches; how the heirloom came to be
hers.

"This is The Wilderness," she told me,
and I believed her, believed the battle
unburied raged on, and I believed I stood
this close, pale in the acoustic shadow,
my disconception safe in her palm.

SKIN DEEP

I can still feel his hard, sharp knees beneath
my bony rump, but I can recall no
stories until the great-aunt gives me his
trunk, its hollow back as humped as his was.
In it, a mouse's long-deserted nest
covers shirt collars still starched; his razor;
strop; shaving brush; fogged tintypes of strangers;
and her brittle love-letters, bound in red
ribbon, their addresses fine blue, bloodless
as the dispassionate cursive on the backs
of her hands; and beneath the letters
his Waterman fountain pen, its lung collapsed.
In the bottom of the trunk, like something
forgotten, long-treasured, or completely
incidental to him, lies the shed
skin of a snake; when I lift it, it rasps,
fragile, transparent, and empty:

One still August night when I was twelve and my three cousins not
much older,
We left the curing barns and slipped away to go skinny-dipping in
Bearskin Creek.
We had a lantern and a stingy half-moon between us; I could barely
make out the white mule
Fog-hobbled on the cooling banks, where we stooped down to untie the
laces of our shoes,
Where I heard again, then again, the sound of fists on the water, and I
whispered, "Wait, boys, wait,"
And swung up the lantern to make out one, then two, then a slew of
them draped in low branches
Against the moon, and their writhing dives to no more evil purpose
than boys who have
Worked too long as men, to no more temptation than not to belly, but
fly blind

Down the sweeter currents of one cooler night. We surrendered it to them
And scrambled back to the hot, infernal crop we had been determined to save.

I lay the snakeskin back where I found it,
fingering its scaled seamlessness to the mute
mouth that has opened wide and released the head
like a tongue, and on that tongue all sense, all
poison, an essential voice telling
itself from its nest of dispossessions.

PRODIGAL

This road is deep now as a riverbed,
mud-packed under a dry, sometime current
of balding tires and hooves. I know if I
had stayed, this new depth would be imperceptible.
My father stands at the end of it, an old
man now, ruts and gullies washed in his face.
Before he can speak, a peacock screams, opens
its blind, repeating eye, and fans me with
a familiar mask. "He is the last of them,"
my father says, "he struts for doves, crows,
the wind." The house behind him lists toward
ruin, toward mistletoe clots in the oak-rot;
on the roof a skew of rods, their green-glass eyes
beg lightning.
"Come on," he says and moves into
and through the stable-gloom. By the rotting harness
and rust-bit I am sure the mare is dead,
but he says not—moon-blind, old, but there—
and points to her, grazing black against
the barbed horizon, beside a thin spring calf.
He's in the middle of tearing down the tractor—
slain, dismembered. An oily ligature
seeps into the ground. "I know I ought
to buy a new one, but I won't," he tells me
as if I don't know he doesn't take well to failure.
"Let's go get us up a supper," he says,
and we walk to the garden's blank plot, but when
he pulls from the ground a ruddy beet, I see
he's planted a crop of roots: turnips, sweet
potatoes grown the color of his hands.
"You don't need teeth for such as these," he laughs,
and moves away from me as if I am
forgiven. I lose my taste for this late
feast; I lose my breath. But there at the edge

of the woods the mushrooms, wild, breathe for me
through dusky gills, and I succumb, follow
him, my fists root-bound and rich with blood.

PLAGUES

A rain crow lusts in the hot, waxy pines.
Day after day a red-tail thirsts against
the flat sky: the field mice dry and dying,
there is nothing worth leaving the thermals.
Tobacco burns in the fields, and corn
smothers in its silk. The cows, blowsy, slow,
brood in the sallow pond, hooves sunk, sucking
silky mud that rises like blood.
                                        "Smitten,
we are smitten with old plagues." The great-aunt
waves her hands, her thin forearms sumac-red
with easy bruises.
                              "Aw, listen to you,"
I humor her, "we are having a drought,
but the almanac—"
                              "—did not predict these
seventeen-year locusts." She's mad now. "'Pharaoh,
Pharaoh,' hear them plead?"
                                        I listen, but hear
wordless their persistent rumor. "I don't know
about that, Aunt Kate; I don't remember
the Bible like you do."
                                  "I would tear out
your tongue like a bloody root," she tells me,
"but I am tired," lays down her head in her
narrow lap. A hymn trembles, rises from
her thighs: *Shall we gather at the river?*

The neighbor cranks the '49 Ford motor
that runs his irrigation pump, faithless:
the fields shoulder the rank beat of wings, wings
of bitter water. All night the orphaned
locusts wheeze in the darkness, grafted now

with disinheritated language, until
we are all of one mind, one swollen tongue:
Pharaoh, Pharaoh, as if there were something
keeping us, as if we could be let go.

TRANSGRESSIONS

I.

He sat in the open doorway. Closed, blank
as any door, he looked at me, and the years
between us distilled down to familiar
disappointment: a pointed, trembling finger,
a raised eyebrow the one loose plank in his face.
A crow panted as if breathless, let down
its sun-white wings; sleeping in the tress
the guineas shimmered like heavy, restless fruit;
a grackle looked past us, its white eye doubtful,
bored with what it had already seen;
and the swamp oak, uprooted by forgotten ice,
leafed out against the ground—a fallen sky—
insistent, too, that all was as before.
On the porch, his old hound lay belly-up,
asleep, and he pulled from behind its ear
a tick—an imperfect pearl, blood-fat—
and considered it before he cast it down
and spoke to me. He knew I was the one
come home to help him stay here, die here, to wish him
dead, to suffer this, my own survival.
And he saw me as his Judas, ordained,
a necessary betrayal; though there would be
no final kiss to mark it, the question was
the selfsame lie because the answer—then
as now unspoken—was known: *Why are you here?*

II.

I was mowing the hay, and the field that had been wind
in hay and braided morning glories lay flat,
dying. I had forgotten how quail panic
before the sickle bar, how a fawn mangles

and still won't move, how a buzzard, having forgotten
nothing, circles—patient for the flesh
strewn with thc grain—how even crows' rejoicing
sounds like despair, might be despair that this is
what there is.
                    I found him slumped over
himself, his left side dead, and I held him
in my arms and prayed—the prayer still sour
in my mouth—for his breath to leave him still as that
breathless noon. But the crows' wings beat against
the sun, against his face, and his chest fell
to rise, measuring the difference
between what was asked and what was given.

III.

He thumped his arm against the arm of his chair—
a sound like knocking snow off wet firewood.
But this bruised, bled like a living thing—
felt nothing. He considered what must be
his own pain as if from a great distance,
then looked at me; my being here was proof
he was alive. I learned his body, bathed him—
withered gut and groin—washed his hands, his face,
his back, his thighs.
                        He told me what he wanted,
his tongue so thick it was another language
we both learned, the words foreign, broad,
familiar as a dream remembered late
in the morning. *Here, come here* like slow oil flowed from his mouth.

IV.

Then in the evenings we sat on the porch to watch
night fall at last from dusk, and he would rhyme
a whippoorwill with a slower, hollow call,
close enough so it would come up—sometimes
close enough for us to see its moon-cast
shadow—forgiving him everything for the lust
in the voice that called from our shared darkness.

BARN CAT

I have heard the talk, how she—accused
of suicide by what she refused—let go
this place and herself. Now we're all here
to divide among us what she has not
already willed away—what mattered most,
or not at all: the sunken house, the brace
of swayed mules, querulous hens, the outbuildings
skeletal, wind-scoured.
                                        Though her root cellar is empty,
the stable still groans, magnificent with hay;
from under it, one of the barn cats, nameless,
staggers and stands. I can see it's been days
dying and isn't done yet: a maggot-burned
dissection bares hipbone, living sinew;
the shank moves with flies. This is no wound, this
rude decay. I know I could go to her
house and find loaded, still leaning behind her
kitchen door, the single-shot .22
and with mercy kill what has refused the place
where animals go to die, kill what has risen
out of resolve, inspired, and moves toward me,
as if toward death, who will not despair
to save her, will not mistake this sudden taming.

GOSSIP

They say I outlived him. With me, they watched
him waste, his muscle fall from him, his bones
rise into the sheet. They saw him laid out,
sent under where there is no worm deep enough
for what still sleeps with me, for that sourceless,
dry skittering in the walls: every night
I still rise into what he called morning;
every morning I drink buttermilk
that was before too thick, too heavy
on my tongue. It took me years to learn
to live with it. Now, what would I drink? When
would I rise? They come visit and talk,
and patient for my story, they tell me
theirs: the high blood, the nerves—mysterious, thrumming
nerves—the sugar, the stillborn and breech birth,
the fallen womb, or—the size of some sweet
fruit—the deep, inoperable tumor.

The horse he had when we married would not
be worked or ridden or harnessed. There were no
rearing hysterics: only the whip
fluent in the air, only a shudder
in the traces—the quiet madness
of refusal. Proud he didn't kill it,
he said many a man would have. It stood
years in the stable. There was no chinking
between the logs, and when the light was right,
I could make out its broken silhouette.
One winter night, I saw it out grazing ice,
its breath the smoke of a dead fire. Beyond it,
the fence swayed, the field gaped as if bewildered
at that brute inability to see
freedom as distance. I despised it,
was glad when it died and he dragged its body

out and burned it. A still day, the smoke rose
and would not leave the pasture.
                                                            There is nothing to tell past
the small bone, sunk in the meat, that lodges
in the throat deeper than pulse, blood, breath, voice.
I have a photograph of our golden
wedding anniversary: we hold the knife,
stainless, over a white cake. I mourn
a photograph of his corpse. Lies, all lies.
Airless as mud, the field still chinks the dark
stall. The wagon's tongue is driven in the dust.

STOIC

He has brought again the dozen fall calves;
they bawl and slide from the cattle-hauler,
but she knows by dusk they'll have found their path
prescribed along the fenceline. By morning
rain will have washed the shit from them, and clean
as from afterbirth, they will travel
the spiraled pasture; stoic, they will learn
to read the sky and know what kneeling down
can save. She sees one has a white heart
figured on its forehead; all carry black
markings on their bodies as if continents
were mapped here, and the charted unknown steams,
shudders, on its ribbed shelf, unnavigable.
Better known, the doe-goat he stakes closer,
then farther; her rope, taut as a compass
needle, sweeps toward the magnetic elsewhere
that lies beyond gnomon fenceposts, beyond
the grid of windrows, beyond the distance
that holds her in coincidence. The scythe
swings against the stable wall, bears the arc
of some skeletal sextant, horizon-dulled,
mirrorless, useless in this rain-fat grass.
She can—she tells him over heavy-laden
supper platters—tell one calf from the others,
but she hears her voice rise with the steam
past its leaving, dissipate into silence,
as the meat, complacent, falls from the bone.

PHOENIX

for CCG

The *whys* are all supposed and of a kind:
lost love, what she fought in the mirror, the change of life.
Perhaps there was no one thing that nestled her finger,
neat, against the trigger, that drove the bullet
in the brain, that mussed at last the hair she'd worn
the same way since 1963.
                                                  We pray
over an urn—even her ashes clean, contained.
She would, by request, cheat the slower worm.
Still, I fear for her what does not burn, and hope
at least she left this place—if self indeed
proved inescapable—the way she would
have left in 1964—behind
the wheel, say, of a Galaxy, a Fury,
a Thunderbird—some long, fast car
on a road writhing in light shed like slow skin
from a perfect moon. Flying, flying, she is
swaddled in white, the ragtop down, her head
thrown back; the wind—fine in her hair—begins
to burn. But she only laughs, floors it, will be gone before
this fire consumes itself in the void from which she rises.

afterword

In 1996 I began to edit the Southern Messenger Poetry series for Louisiana State University Press, selecting two books for publication each year. *Pharaoh, Pharaoh,* the first poetry collection by Claudia Emerson (then Andrews), soon appeared. Seven more of her books would follow, with the third, *Late Wife,* winning the Pulitzer Prize and the eighth, *Claude before Time and Space,* coming out in 2018, four years after her death at age fifty-seven. Emerson's poetry generated such an enthusiastic audience that an omnibus collection seemed necessary. But this poet made selecting such a collection difficult. She invariably composed poems in sequences; her books were what I might call "continuities." Her manuscripts came with spaces reserved for poems, often titled, she planned to include but had not yet written. Those poems always arrived for publication. An argument can be made that the eight books form a single entity, but as editor I have made selections here that violate that singularity in favor of an evolving representation. Readers should seek her books, all still in print, for the fullest experience of her poetry, but I hope they find *Ungrafted: New and Selected Poems* to be a substantial show of her accomplishment. It includes twenty-six of her forty known previously uncollected poems, a few of which I amended to reflect Emerson's characteristic voice, style, or intention. "Learning to Dive," for example was written in duple stanzas, but there were also triplets and single lines. I print it in regularized couplets.

Prior to making the selection of poems for this volume, I asked for and received advisory readings of Claudia Emerson's complete poetry from poets Fred Chappell (her teacher), Kate Daniels, Ron Smith, David Wojahn, and Ellen Bryant Voigt. My choices were informed by both their affirmations and dissents. To each I offer my gratitude. To Kent Ippolito, Claudia's husband, without whose help this book would not be possible, our great thanks. To Claudia, a woman wise and wonderful in her art, I say what I always said in accepting her manuscripts: "Thank you for the awesome poems and for your faith in the Southern Messenger Poetry series. It is a great pleasure to be your editor now and forever."

DAVE SMITH

notes

“Red Sam in the Days That Follow”: The line *“But nobody’s killed,” June Star said with disappointment . . .* is from “A Good Man Is Hard to Find,” by Flannery O’Connor.

“Pitty Sing in Arms”: The line *Her son, Bailey, didn’t like to arrive at a motel with a cat* is from “A Good Man Is Hard to Find.”

“Lucynell in Heaven”: The line beginning *The body, lady, is like a house* is from “The Life You Save May Be Your Own,” by Flannery O’Connor.

“Joy in the Loft”: The line beginning *Whenever she looked at Joy this way* is from “Good Country People,” by Flannery O’Connor.

“L’Inconnue de la Seine”: “The Unknown Woman of the Seine” was a sixteen-year-old woman who drowned in the Seine River in Paris. Her beauty compelled an attending pathologist to have a face mask made. The mask subsequently made famous an image of a woman both unknown and mysterious as beauty itself. In turn, the mask became associated with artists and poets, as a kind of muse, an image often hung in their homes and workplaces. In 1966 it was employed in making the first training doll for CPR rescues.

about the author

Before her death in 2014, Claudia Emerson was professor of English and a member of the creative writing faculty at Virginia Commonwealth University. Emerson served as poet laureate of Virginia and won numerous awards for teaching and writing, including the 2006 Pulitzer Prize for Poetry for her collection *Late Wife*. Other books by Emerson include *Pharaoh, Pharoah* (1997), *Pinion* (2002), *Figure Studies* (2008), *Secure the Shadow* (2012), *The Opposite House* (2015), *Impossible Bottle* (2015), and *Claude before Time and Space* (2018).